The Making Of A Drum Company

The Autobiography Of
William F. Ludwig II

edited by Rob Cook

ISBN 1-888408-05-7

Published by Rebeats Publications
www.Rebeats.com
219 Prospect, P.O. Box 6, Alma, Michigan 48801
989-463-4757   fax 989-463-6545   rebeats@rebeats.com

Dedication

To my beautiful and supportive wife Marguerite, our children and grandchildren.

To the percussion community that my family has had the pleasure to serve for nearly a century. The hobbyists. The students. The professionals. The virtuosos!

LUDWIG FAMILY TREE

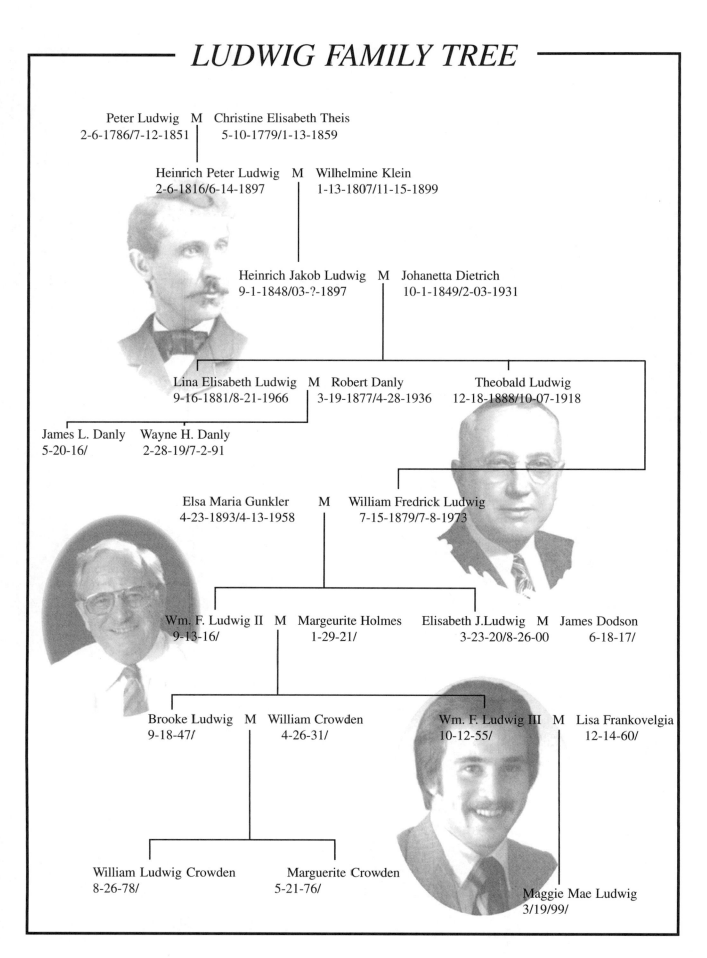

Peter Ludwig   M   Christine Elisabeth Theis
2-6-1786/7-12-1851   5-10-1779/1-13-1859

Heinrich Peter Ludwig   M   Wilhelmine Klein
2-6-1816/6-14-1897   1-13-1807/11-15-1899

Heinrich Jakob Ludwig   M   Johanetta Dietrich
9-1-1848/03-?-1897   10-1-1849/2-03-1931

Lina Elisabeth Ludwig   M   Robert Danly
9-16-1881/8-21-1966   3-19-1877/4-28-1936

Theobald Ludwig
12-18-1888/10-07-1918

James L. Danly   Wayne H. Danly
5-20-16/   2-28-19/7-2-91

Elsa Maria Gunkler   M   William Fredrick Ludwig
4-23-1893/4-13-1958   7-15-1879/7-8-1973

Wm. F. Ludwig II   M   Margeurite Holmes
9-13-16/   1-29-21/

Elisabeth J. Ludwig   M   James Dodson
3-23-20/8-26-00   6-18-17/

Brooke Ludwig   M   William Crowden
9-18-47/   4-26-31/

Wm. F. Ludwig III   M   Lisa Frankovelgia
10-12-55/   12-14-60/

William Ludwig Crowden   Marguerite Crowden
8-26-78/   5-21-76/

Maggie Mae Ludwig
3/19/99/

Table of Contents

The Making Of A Drum Company

The Autobiography of William F. Ludwig II

Heritage

In 1886 my grandfather, Henry Jakob Ludwig, left Germany with his family and struck out for the New World.

The birthplace of Wm. F. Ludwig Sr., Nenderoth, Germany. The village of Nenderoth is 60 miles north of Frankfurt, in the Rhine River Valley.

He became part of the great migration wave of the later part of the 19th century. The Ludwigs landed in New York City where friends and fellow musicians awaited to steer Henry Ludwig to work in his profession as a trombonist.

These plans were torpedoed by the New York Musician's Union which ruled that there must be a waiting period of one year before new arrivals could work in the music business. So much for overseas planning! In dismay, Henry called friends in the German community in Chicago and they assured him there was no waiting period there, and the cost to join was only $1.00. What a buy!

The Ludwigs left New York without playing a note and trained to Chicago where in the heart of the German community Heinrich Jakob Ludwig set up his family of three, with one more son still to come. It proved to be the ideal location to begin life anew even though no one in the family spoke a word of English!

The elder Ludwig immediately got work through contacts because of his ability as a talented trombonist. Thanks to experience gained in the German Military Bands, he was an excellent reader which meant he could play all types of music. (It was to spare his son, William Frederick Ludwig, that same cruel and exhausting two-

year compulsory military service in 1870 that prompted him to flee to the New World.)

The Ludwigs settled into a rented wooden house on 14th street near Halsted Avenue in 1886. The children, Lina Elizabeth, William, and later Theobald, were all enrolled in the German school in the neighborhood and promptly learned English as a second language.

As newcomers in that school, they were often taunted. William had all the buttons ripped from his brand new suit the first week. Gradually the family blended into the community and father Henry found enough work in the music community to support his family and arrange for music lessons for William and Theobald.

Dental care in those days was extremely rudimentary– when you had a toothache you pulled the tooth and that was that. Henry had lost some teeth already which caused a weakening of the support a brass player needs to form a strong embrochure. He knew this could only get worse so he resolved to school his sons in any instrument but wind instruments.That left three choices– piano, violin, and drums. Naturally both boys started on the violin. There was plenty of work for violinists, thus their earning ability would be large indeed.

After two years both boys had had enough of fiddling and simply rebelled– to the utter disgust of their father. No musical training was provided for the eldest Ludwig child, Lina. As a girl she was expected to marry young, be supported by her husband, and have children.

Since the boys refused to practice, the teacher quit and left father Ludwig to move along to the next non-wind instrument– the piano. The piano was a perfect choice because it taught the bass clef as well as the treble clef. A teacher was hired to come to the house and a piano had to be purchased. The piano set Henry back $35.00– nearly a month's wages in those days! Again Pop was frustrated as two years later first Theobald and then William announced they were finished with the piano lessons. Father was again furious. All was not lost, however, since the four years of musical study, however fitful, provided the embryo for what was to follow in the political campaign of 1889.

William Jennings Bryan was running for President of the country on the free silver ticket. There was a torch-light parade through the Ludwig neighborhood and William was there sharing in the excitement as he marched alongside the drum and bugle corps of the Illinois Na-

Elsa and Little Billy (the author), age 2

Ludwig & Ludwig and played nights in the percussion section of the Chicago Symphony Orchestra. Mother, Elsa, had been a lyric soprano in the Chicago Grand Opera Company where she met father who was the principal percussionist about 1912. They were married June 1, 1914 and honeymooned in The Congress Hotel across the street from the Auditorium Theater on Congress Street so they wouldn't miss rehearsals and performances. When I came along in 1916, mother retired

Elsa's wedding dress, June 1, 1914

tional Guard all the way to the end of the parade. He was fascinated with the drummers and inquired of their instructor, George Cattlet.

The next day William Ludwig announced to anyone of the family who would listen that he wanted to become a drummer. Since this fit Henry's initial requirement of a non-wind instrument, a drum William would have, and lessons from the Guard Instructor George Cattlet. Thus a career was born– not only that of a great percussionist but the foremost drum builder of that entire century!

I was born September 13, 1916, in the Robert Burns Hospital on Washington Boulevard in Chicago, just a half block west of Garfield Park. It is long gone, converted to a parking lot. My interest in fine literature could have come from my place of birth, for Robert Burns was one of Scotland's greatest poets!

My earliest recollections are of peering through crib posts on sunny afternoons in the back room of our apartment in Rogers Park on Touhy Avenue about 1918. It was summertime and breezes wafted lazily through the lightly curtained windows. Dad worked at the drum plant

from the opera company to devote full time to motherhood.

Ludwig & Ludwig was growing, so father resigned from the Symphony in 1918 to devote all of his energies to drum making. There must have been enough money rolling in to allow to pay sufficient salaries to both Ludwigs– my father, and his younger brother by eight years, Theobald Ludwig.

My father's brother, Theo (Ted), was an im-

Theobald Ludwig in 1916, age 28

portant part of the Ludwig & Ludwig drum company. When America became involved in World War I in April 1917 the government moved quickly to manage the economy by identifying scarce materials and placing restrictions on their use for nonessential items. Since drums were quickly identified as nonessential to the war effort,brass, steel, copper and other metals were banned to drum companies. The company changed over to rope tensioned drums.

One very large bid was under consideration and in anticipation of getting that order my father and Theo purchased all the iron hooks needed for the 400 field drums. The order went to the Fred Gretsch Company of Brooklyn, New York. Theo was sent East to find out why. He found that the bid had been changed from fifteen inch diameter shells to fifteen and a half– a size Ludwig could not make. In an effort to find out why the change, Theo looked up the Government chief in charge of all musical instrument purchases; one Colonel Brockenshire at the Philahelphia Quartermaster Depot. Theo went there only to learn that Brockenshire was caught up in the influenza epidemic of that year and confined to the influenza ward of the Government hospital.

Somehow, Theobald got into that ward and found from Brockenshire that the Gretsch Company, in collusion with a local jobber from New York City, Buegeleisen & Jacobson, had convinced the army that the larger diameter on a field drum was better in producing volume than the fifteen inch. Theobald had solved the dilemma and made plans to return to Chicago and his brother to spread the news. Since he had the afternoon until train time he called on a local dealer there in Philadelphia who took one look at him and said "Man, you're sick. You better get back as soon as possible. You look like you have caught the flu." That dealer called my father that night to alert him to meet the train in the morning. My father did just that and was appalled to find Theo running a very high fever and unable to even get off the train. An ambulance was sent for but it was of no use, for young Theobald Ludwig died within four days.

My father was, of course, devastated. One half of Ludwig and Ludwig was gone, and at the early age of only 29! My father related this story to me for the rest of his life and placed his portrait of Theo in the pages of many future Ludwig catalogs.

Although the order never came, I have always drawn inspiration from Theo's effort to save a lost order and it has inspired me to go the extra mile in many a business deal since then.

Evanston, Illinois – 1924

Though my father had resigned from the Symphony and the Opera Company to devote all of his efforts to the growing drum business, he continued to play, as a serious amateur. He joined the Shrine in order to play with the great Medina Brass Band and enlarge his con-

The Ludwig homestead in Evanston– 1924

tacts with the business community of Chicago. About this time he received a call from A.R. McAllistar, director of the prize-winning Joliet High School Band. This was a key call in his and my life. McAllister said his drummers were the weakest section of his band and asked if my father could come out to Joliet to help out. Joliet is only around forty miles from Chicago but in 1922 it was a day's drive round trip due to the very poor roads. It was, therefore, at some sacrifice, that my father loaded up the car with practice pads which were newly developed, drum sticks, and drum methods, such as they were, and headed out for Joliet. When he arrived he was appalled at the poor quality of the section. No two drummers had their drums set up at anywhere near a correct playing angle and no two held the drum sticks correctly. He spent the entire day with that section and improved their performance tremendously. This was the first drum clinic in percussion history, but more than that, it gave him an idea– why not participate in drum education on a company level? Thus, the kernel of an idea was born which later led to his formation of the National Association of Rudimental Drummers– the N.A.R.D. and standardizing the rudimental system of drumming.

Evanston

In 1922 my parents picked out a corner lot in Evanston, at 1001 Maple Street, and built a brick colonial three-story house on it. We moved in the following year from Rogers Park. My sister Bettie was with us, having been born on March 23, 1920. Among my earliest tasks as an eight year old were to mow the lawn in the summer, shovel snow in the winter, and crank the heating oil from the underground storage tank into the indoor feeding tank to the furnace. This activity lasted about a half hour a week depending on the weather and I am sure that being right handed built up my right arm muscle tone!

Shortly after moving in my father brought home a practice pad mounted on a drum stand (one of the first produced) and a big instruction book and a huge pair of drum sticks, set it all up in my bedroom and announced that my drum lessons would begin that moment. "What fun," I thought. Each evening after supper, which was

always on the table at six o'clock, it was up to my bedroom to work out on that rubber-covered block of wood. The novelty soon wore off (in about a week) and I started skipping some practice periods. My father soon caught on and raised hell which led to tears and wailing. I went to my mother for protection. She told Dad to lay off. He told her in no uncertain terms to stay out of it and the lessons resumed, this time on a daily basis. Thus for half an hour every night it was da-da-ma-ma-da-da-ma-ma..... left left right right and at a very slow deliberate cadence. Most dull and boring, believe me! Often I would attempt to increase the tempo but Dad would slow me back down to a monotonous *even* cadence. It was explained to me that what I was working on was the long roll. Rudiment number one. The most basic of the rudiments of drumming and that it had to be learned right or not at all. Slowly, slowly the cadence

4th of July, 1926 (L-R) cousin James C. Danly (son of Ludwig's greatest engineer R.C. Danly), cousin Herman Gunkler (who rose to play in famous dance bands such as Kay Kyser), Wm. F. Ludwig II with his first drum, Wayne Danly (who became an airline pilot), and sister Bettie, flag bearer

was quickened but only when it was even hand to hand.

In about two months I was performing twice as fast as I had begun, but the effort was exhausting not to mention boring. My father wouldn't quit and drilled me each night after dinner on that gum rubber pad a half hour daily. Finally, in the third month, I requested a promotion to a drum because I was getting sick of the smell of gum rubber. To this day I can recognize it and still hate it! Dad turned me down, saying I had to learn more rudiments before he would bring home a drum. Imagine it! Here was one of the largest producers of drums in the world turning out hundreds of drums daily and would he bring his eight-year-old son one? No, sir!

speeding up so much that the beatings became uneven.

After Christmas, 1923 came a new year and more rudiments. I had finally reached the forlorn conclusion that I would have to learn all twenty-six rudiments before I would get that drum! Finally in the summer of 1924 (one year after that first agonizing lesson), I was half way through to my objective. Still no drum. Eight months later, in March of 1925, I tackled No. 26 and got my drum... a 10-inch deep shell fourteen inches in diameter, single tension, calf heads, with sticks and sling to match! That drum had a plain mahogany finish but still I was so proud of it that I played it for any visitors who came to our house. Having spent two years on that gum rubber practice pad I was now ready for some drum cadences. But first came marching with it. My father showed me how to sling up

Ludwig family portrait in the year 1922. Sister Bettie, mother Elsa, the author age 6, father Wm. F. Ludwig Sr.

Not until I mastered more rudiments than the long roll! A man who had seemed so kind and loving– my father– had become in my eyes a monster– my worst enemy. In the summer time the boys in my neighborhood were outside playing ball and calling for me after supper but no, I had to keep lifting and dropping those big heavy sticks.... da-da-ma-ma-da-da-ma-ma until my arms and wrists ached. Finally, toward Christmas time, I was performing more like a steam locomotive. And to my surprise, the beatings were nice and even. A tinge of pride now began to creep into my practice sessions and I no longer needed daily practice supervision. Did I get a reward? No, I got another rudiment! The flam. Very patiently my father guided the sticks in my first flams. High hand hits hard, low hand lightly. Then change hands, right high, left low. And so on.. I must admit the flam came rather easily but still each practice session began and closed with running down the long roll at least twice, open, close and open but never

The author, Age 6

5

with the drum at the proper angle resting on the left knee. It was important not to let the drum slip off sideways which sharply changed the angle of the head causing the right stick bead to dig into the calf head and often tear it. Since the drum was very light weight, (I was ten at the time), it was difficult to march and balance it on the left knee. From this experience my father conceived a leg rest to steady the drum on the march. He had his engineers make a model up and brought the first sample home for me to try and it worked. But it could not be folded for storage with a canvas cover covering the drum. Back to the shop it went where further tinkering in the engineering department created a clever folding hinge with an on-lock and an off-lock which became most sought after world-wide. Hundreds of thousands were produced and sold and copied by every drum company that existed at that time and later as well.

My first complete piece was of course the standard roll-off, followed in short order by the standard 2/4 and 6/8. I joined the Boy Scouts of America and played in

The author at Culver Military Academy

the Evanston chapter Drum and Bugle Corps. Naturally my solid rudimental training gave me the advantage and I was soon appointed drum master of the ten man drum section. I worked out various routines on the march and signals indicating changes from 2/4 to 6/8 rhythms.

All went well until one fateful day in the summer of 1926. My mother gravely announced that I was to take piano lessons! "Good grief," I thought. "What next?" And before I could muster up a defense, the piano teacher was at the door one Saturday morning!

He was a very neatly attired young man and I hated him on sight. I just didn't want piano lessons! But my father backed up my mother and I could see that defiance would only cut into my play time. They thought I should get acquainted with the treble clef as well as the bass clef which is the drum clef. We had a mahogany finish Steinway baby grand piano prominently situated in the bay window of our living room so that the neighbors could not miss it and see that we were a family of culture and not just a bunch of ruffian drummers. My baby sister Bettie also got roped in and her half hour lesson on Saturday mornings followed mine. My father liked the idea of both of us suffering lessons, as he could see some return on his piano investment. Being four years older, my progress on the scales was much faster than hers and gave me an advantage which I used to taunt her unmercifully. Saturday became the most dreaded day of the week. Friday was the cram day for both of us, so a system of whose turn it was on the piano was refereed by mother.

After several weeks on the circle of fifths, I was given a piece. It could have been *Row, Row, Row Your Boat*, I don't recall, but the fact that I could produce some melody and harmony began to appeal to me. I am certain this revelation occurs to everyone tackling the mastery of any musical instrument. Six months or so performing for house guests provides a satisfying sensation of accomplishment. A dividend of sorts. In my case, however, the piano study was preparing me for a later day when I would be confronted with many percussion instruments to master other than just the field drum. I was being grounded in music, harmony, and rhythm– the three elements of music.

Culver Military Academy– Summer 1927

In my eleventh year I had the opportunity to spend a summer at the Culver Military Academy summer camp program at Culver, Indiana. At the end of June I was packed off with my drum sticks and pad to the Academy. I loved it! Each day was filled with new experiences and lessons in woodcrafts, camping, boating, and of course the drum and bugle corps. Each evening all six hundred boys in the camp assembled in their dress uniforms on the parade grounds to pass in review before visitors. The cannon on the hill fired the evening salute and the Nation's colors were gently lowered while the entire corps of cadets stood at attention and hand salute. All except we drummers who maintained a steady fortissimo roll. My love of the military customs was born at Culver. Learning and performing the routines in the Culver drum and bugle corps sharpened my hand technique and strong sense of rhythmic cadence.

Back home I threw myself into renewed piano and drum practice. Lessons continued on both. There was no school band to play in during those early years so the Boy Scouts had to make up for it. The following year, 1928, I returned to Culver Military Academy and took charge of the drum section again. I had Dad ship down twelve gum rubber pads mounted on angled blocks and attached them to a ten foot table so we could practice our cadences and routines together without disturbing the camp. Slowly my enthusiasm for drumming and music in general was building and I looked forward to playing in the band!

I was old enough by this time to enjoy going to the

(l-r) Sister Bettie, Mother, the author,
in a garden pose, Evanston, 1928

drum plant with my father on Saturdays. In those days the work week was a full six eight-hour days. I had the run of the office and factory and saw how drum sticks were turned and shells laid up and bent. We visited the tannery on Elston Avenue which I disliked intensely because the odors were nearly intolerable. Every day hundreds of animal skins, mostly calf skins, were dropped off on the factory floor... All smelly, slimy, and often bloody. In the summers the flies were there, too– in the millions! My father did not approve of my distaste for the tannery. He always maintained it was a delightful odor because it was the odor of *business* and the drum business was good business.

Also on Saturdays at the plant I discovered the banjo school located on the third floor. Ludwig & Ludwig entered the banjo manufacturing business in the twenties because the banjo was the most popular fretted instrument in the whole music world. The banjo business enabled the tannery to use up the smallest calf skins as well as the trimmings or corners left over from the regular bass drum sizes. Robert Danly, my father's brother-in-law and chief engineer designed and built the largest (and by far the most expensive) piece of equipment Ludwig ever had; a multi-router capable of carving out ten banjo necks at a time! It's cost was astronomical but it was extremely efficient and enabled the company to exist on a competitive footing with crosstown neighbor the Slingerland Banjo Company at Belden and Wayne Avenues.

Unfortunately for Ludwig & Ludwig, the banjo craze was already tapering off and Slingerland was aroused to a terrible resolve; to retaliate by getting into the drum business. They too had a tannery and wanted to use up all their inventory of raw skins the same as Ludwig. As I said, I had the run of the factory at age thirteen and so I discovered the banjo school on the third floor and met the genial head of the school, Mr. Charlie MacNeil. He was a man of great personality, and of course a supurb banjo player himself. He was a promoter and had convinced Ludwig & Ludwig to set up not only the banjo school but mail-order lesson plans as well.

The Charlie MacNeil Banjo School, a division of Ludwig & Ludwig at 1611-27 N. Lincoln (later Wolcott Avenue), became nationally famous and was responsible for turning out hundreds of fine banjoists from coast to coast. I was able to spend many happy Saturdays as I entered my teens not only observing the manufacture of drums but banjos as well.

The problem with Danly's marvelous neck router was that it turned out in one day a full weeks inventory of necks and then sat idle for the rest of the week. Economists would criticize such a multi-router as too expensive for the purpose. Since the public was becoming tired of the banjo, the sales began to taper off.

Ludwig & Ludwig enjoyed their first one million dollar year in 1926. The following year, 1927, saw about the same sales volume and there existed a very great optimism throughout the organization. A massive building program under the supervision of Mr. Danly had been launched and completed by 1923 which more than doubled the size of the factory. Two sons of Mr. Danly joined the engineering department– George and Philo Danly. The three Danlys turned out mechanical inventions of such stupendous originality that Ludwig & Ludwig easily captured the lead in sales and approval of the drumming fraternity. My father had only to describe to the Danly engineering team what the drummer would like to have for his tools and they created the answer with their magical strokes of engineering drawings and metal magic. So massive and advanced were their designs that most are still in use today and have been copied by every drum company almost one hundred years later. This era 1921 through 1931 was truly the great era of drum inventions and can easily be said to have been the birth of the modern percussion industry as we know it today. There I was, a boy, in the middle of it!

Sound Pictures Kill Off Vaudeville

On October 27, 1927, a monumental, earth-shaking event occured which changed the lives and habits of millions of people around the world..... the first talking pictures. Immediately the picture show houses rushed to equip themselves with the electrical magic to produce talking films in their theaters and eliminate live musicians from the pit. From coast to coast in the next twelve months, 18,000 drummers were thrown out of work!

The effect on the drum company was devastating. Sales plummeted. Of the 350 employees in the drum plant and tannery, half were discharged in that first year.

I felt it too as Saturday work was eliminated, ending my visits to the drum factory as well as the MacNeil Banjo School. In 1929 the banjo school was closed. I noticed a melancholy air descending on our household. Vacation trips were curtailed and I could tell something bad was happening. What it was I didn't know.

I saw my first talking picture in 1928 (Al Jolson in black face as "The Jazz Singer"). We all went down to the Chicago Theater on State Street. The lines were long at the ticket office. The wait was about an hour. After we were admitted the first thing I noticed was a great many people standing in the aisle just frozen and staring at the moving film with words coming from the lips of the actors. Some in the audience even attempted to get behind the screen to see where that sound was coming from! The second thing I noticed was that the pit was empty. No lights from the music stands, no musicians, no conductor. And yet there was music. Where it came from we didn't know. Finally, in our seats, we were delightfully entertained through the next two hours with a feature film, a newsreel, and a comedy. We drove home in silence. Mom sat in front with Dad, who drove; sister Bettie and I were in the back seat. No one talked until near home my father said, "This is the end," and my mother began to cry.

There were few school bands in the 1920s so there were few drum sales to schools. In the grade school, middle school, and first year of Evanston High School there was no music department at all, so the only drumming open to me was still the Boy Scouts. But still my drum practice and some instruction, and, of course, the

William F Ludwig II and William F. Ludwig III with the Roy Knapp theatre-type kit that became obsolete in 1927. This set now is on display in the Percussive Arts Society Museum in Lawton, Oklahoma.

piano lessons continued. I noticed my father more and more detached as if wrapped in a huge thought and I didn't understand unless it could be the business problems which never left him. (That is the way it is with every business owner.)

C.G. Conn, Ltd. To The Rescue!

By 1930 business was so bad because of the Vitaphone (as the new sound pictures were called) and the general economic despair caused by the stock market crash of October, 1929, that my father decided to follow U.G. Leedy's move of the previous year and sell his beloved company to the C.G. Conn company of Elkhart, Indiana. The Conn company was the world's largest manufacturer of band instruments, turning out one thousand instruments per day. Charles Greenleaf was president and owner of the majority stock, having purchased it in 1915 from the founder, Colonel Charles Girard Conn. Mr. Greenleaf was an astute operator acquiring businesses at bargain prices when they were at a low ebb. Since their drum manufacturing division was very incomplete they had purchased the Leedy Drum Company for cash and moved it lock, stock, and barrel to Elkhart the year before. The Leedy tannery was located behind the sprawling band instrument factory and the drum assembly and manufacturing was done in the west half of the Beuscher Band Instrument plant on Jackson Avenue.

My father approached Mr. Greenleaf in a very weakened position in the spring of 1930, and at a luncheon meeting turned over Ludwig & Ludwig stock for C.G. Conn stock in the face amount of nearly $1,000,000.00, which relieved him of his considerable distress. Even though the terms contained the provision that Ludwig's production would remain on Lincoln street, the Conn executives moved everything into the Beuscher plant on Jackson Avenue in Elkhart six months after

Conn's Elkhart building that housed both Leedy and Ludwig & Ludwig drum production.

the papers were signed. Business continued to deteriorate– as did the Conn stock. The stock had dropped from it's original face value of $1,000,000.00 down to only $100,000.00 by 1935, so it began to seem that my dad sold his company very cheaply!

One can only conjecture about the wisdom of Mr. Greenleaf's moves at that time considering the sagging business in the music industry generally. I suppose having the leading drum companies under one roof would allow them to capture a dominant share of the percussion market and they did for sure.

School bands were organizing throughout the land and Mr. Greenleaf invested heavily in the movement, particularly with the National Music Camp which Joe Maddy had organized at Interlochen, Michigan, in 1927. Conn had been giving the bulk of the background instruments to the camp at the beginning of each summer including the first aluminum bass fiddles ever made. They were so immune to moisture that the students used to float them in Lake Maxinkochie!

Elkhart, Indiana–
The Band Instrument Capital of The World:
Here We Come!

In the spring of 1931 we moved from Evanston, Illinois, to Elkhart, Indiana, at the orders of the new owners, the C.G. Conn Company. My father was assigned to the drum division as titular head of Ludwig & Ludwig reporting alongside George Way who was head of the Leedy division all in the Beuscher building in Elkhart. I enrolled in the Elkhart High School and played in the band and orchestra. This was my first experience playing in large musical organizations of ninety or more players.

My route home from the high school took me past the Beuscher building and I often stopped to observe manufacturing and sometimes to pick up much needed accessories for the school. One day while walking down Main Street, I passed the local music store and was suddenly arrested by the sounds of the storm section of the *Poet and Peasant Overture*. This furious music really turned me on! I beseeched my parents to purchase not only the recording but the tall standup RCA machine itself. Father was reluctant to lay out the $100.00 neccessary, but mother again came to the rescue and that machine was delivered the next day. I promptly wore that record out!

The Wainwright Band Camp was nearby and I was enrolled in the summer of 1931 as a percussionist in a fine concert band of that era directed by the remarkable organizer and conductor Jack Wainwright. Three private lessons per week were included and my reading ability improved greatly. I moved to first chair in the percussion section. We worked up such numbers as Sibeliu's overture *Finlandia* and many marches, taking this repertoire on the road to nearby towns where we often set up on temporary stages in the middle of streets.

The girls flocked around "backstage" and we showed off for them since percussionists were singled out by the girls for particular adulation. This is true throughout the thousand or so years of musical history, for drumming is as close to an athletic competition as you can get and certainly more active and exciting than any of the other instruments in the band. Of course having my parents come to the camp near LaGrange, Indiana, for Sunday afternoon concerts puffed me up plenty. I am sure they appreciated my progress.

Elkhart High School

That fall of 1931 awakened my interest in playing in both the band as well as the orchestra at the Elkhart High School. My lessons and playing experience at the Wainwright band camp had improved both my technique and desire to advance in the percussion sections in both organizations. I wanted to be timpanist who is, of course, recognized as the king of the percussion section! In addition, there were openings in the band for soloists for the fall, Christmas, and spring concerts in the huge main auditorium. So I practiced xylophone solos within the band's repertoire such as the *Brahams Fifth and Sixth Hungarian Dances* and *Nola*. Also there were spring solo drum contests to prepare for, so I was plenty busy.

The Bell Lyra

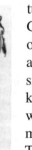

The bell lyra had its beginnings two centuries ago in German military bands as the Glockenspiel. It consisted of a single row of bars mounted vertically on a frame. This alignment left room for only ten bars and since the marches were written in various keys a system of interchangeability of bars was worked out. The player carried eight more bars in a special pouch on his belt. The bars were hooked on the rails of the frame. As the key signature changed, certain natural bars were unhooked and placed in the pouch and replaced with the appropriate chromatic bars thus covering the key signature of the march. Since the left hand had to carry the lyra, the right hand struck the notes. Thus only two strokes per measure were possible on the march but this was enough to carry the melody– usually the piccolo part. The weight of the steel bars and frame German Glockenspiel was

Chromatic Bell Lyra

considerable, but easily handled by a German soldier. However, my father realized this could represent an obstacle to school marching band sales so he used an aluminum frame with a double row of aluminum bars; there were twenty-five in all, covering one and a half octaves and weighing less than half the German glockenspiel. He had to sell his masters, the C.G. Conn company and its chairman Charlie D. Greenleaf, on his bell lyra, as he called it. To do this he enlisted me, since I was a member of the local high school band. To get started I wrote out the bell parts for every march in the Elkhart High School Library that would be used on the march and at football games. I combined the piccolo parts in C with the B-flat cornet parts in B-flat transposed

The author in the Elkhart band, 1932

into C of course, and just two notes to be played to the bar. This was enough to carry the melody. I would like to point out that I was able to transpose the bell parts because of my early piano training for which I thank my mother. Mr. Greenleaf came to some of the games and, thus, was exposed to his first marching lyra prototype. In addition, my father took one to the Shrine convention in Toronto and urged the Conn officials to listen to the great parade of the Shriners at their national convention in the fall of 1932 and the bells came through loud and clear over the radio airways. Between my father's exposure and my playing in front of the football band, we were able to convince the Conn executives that here was a product that readily fit into every band's marchng program. Production of the twenty-five bar aluminum bell lyra was finally ordered in January of the following year, 1934.

Spring Competition– Contests!

In the spring of 1933, I finally achieved the concert band position of timpanist. That was indeed a proud day for me. There is only one timpanist in every musical organization and this requires utmost attention at all times and especially careful pitch tuning in every composition. The spring season at Elkhart High School was also very busy. Most of the student body was in a band, orchestra, or choir since Elkhart, Indiana, was the band and orchestra capital of the world. Each spring we were required to apply for a solo audition to compete in the regional and state-wide competitions. And, of course, this meant that all three musical units of the school had to prepare for competition as well. In the band we worked up Rossini's *William Tell* overture as well as Wagner's *Reinzi.* Both had prominent percussion parts including several timpani solos. Since I did so well in the band I was appointed timpanist in the orchestra. My cup runneth over! I practiced so hard! I worked up *The Downfall of Paris* from the Moeller Book and entered the solo snare drum competitive classification. The Moeller Book was compiled in 1925 by Gus Moeller and my father and published in that year. I recall many smoky Sunday afternoons at our house in Evanston watching these two great authorities standing at our dining room table with practice pads and manuscript spread out all over the table. They were great drummers and cigar smokers! The Moeller Book was then published by Ludwig & Ludwig

The author as a hot shot high-schooler, 1933.

Inc. It standardized the rudiments into 26 rudiments.

The drum competition requirements called for, in addition to a solo, three rudiments: long roll, flam, and paradiddle open, closed, and open again. At the Ft. Wayne regional competitions, I came in first. The same for state contests in Evansville, Indiana. And finally at the National competitions held on the campus of Northwestern University that year: first place, best in the nation! I made my parents so proud, particularly my father, for he could see the results at last of his good solid rudimental foundation of nine years previously. I felt, "Now I am on my way!" It was also the beginning of a first-class ego!

National drum champion, 1933

The National Music Camp, Interlochen, Michigan

In the summer of 1933 I was enrolled at the prestigious National Music Camp at Interlochen, Michigan near Traverse City. The country is beautiful up there, with many lakes and fragrant pines bending in the breezes. The camp was artfully located between two lakes. The performing stage outdoors was constructed using huge tree trunks from the forest and opened onto a vast open-air bowl-shaped auditorium All performances of the high school band and orchestra took place at this location. After settling into my assigned cabin where I would live for the next eight weeks I reported Tuesday morning to the bowl for the first orchestra rehearsal at 9:00 A.M. There I met the members of the percussion section and awaited an assignment. The piece on the music stand was strange to me. It was Tschaikowsky's Fifth Symphony and I had never heard of either Tschaikowsky or his fifth symphony. One of the older percussionists who introduced himself to me as Fred Fennell was a repeat camper from two years previously. He took charge of the section by stepping behind the pair of Ludwig & Ludwig balanced action timpani and played the entire symphony straight through and on only two timpani– a part written for four timps! It was the most amazing thing I had ever seen or heard. Fennell played through the entire symphony from beginning to end without missing a note or being out of tune (as near as I could tell). By 10:00 A.M. that morning , the first of the summer, I knew I wasn't so hot as a timpanist. At Elkhart the most difficult pieces we played were *The Merry Wives of Windsor, The Poet And Peasant Overture*, and *William Tell,* which were all two-timpani parts not nearly as complicated as the Tschaiwosky Fifth Symphony. I knew I had more than met my match in the brilliant young Frederick Fennell and I also knew that I would spend the rest of the summer in awe of his mighty prowess at the timps. It was a great awakening but that's what music camps are all about– the chance to see the best talent in the nation. I studied Fennell's every move and the few times I got a shot at it I tried to play up to his level. Mostly I spent eight weeks playing bass drum and snare drum in both band as well as orchestra because there was no question who was boss– it was Fennell!

He was a very good teacher; kind and patient, and that helped smooth over all the shock that I wasn't the greatest percussionist in the world after all! In addition we had a percussion coach from the Cleveland Symphony Orchestra, one Frank Tichy, who schooled me with weekly lessons on the percussion parts we were playing in both band and orchestra. In both of these organizations we enjoyed the wonderful exposure of

Fred Fennell tuning up for a performance at Interlochen in 1933

one rehearsal and one preformance per week.

One week we found the *Anvil Chorus* from Verdi's opera *Il Trovatore* on the stands. George saw this as an opportunity to star. From somewhere he produced two full-size anvils on stands. He supplied me with a battery-charged wire brush which I scraped across the surface of the anvil at the same instant I struck the anvil with a pretty good-sized blacksmith's hammer. The sparks were dramatic and flew into the air in all directions. George had the same setup and we were positioned at the front of the band on either side. We wore leather aprons from the head tannery to deflect the sparks and leather gloves to protect our hands. The effect was very dramatic and the audience couldn't get enough. We played many encores of *Il Trovatore's Anvil Chorus*! I always considered that setup typical of George's fertile brain.

guest conductors of national recognition who made us play above our heads. The summer was well spent in igniting within my breast a burning desire to play professionally, so I practiced every free hour there was in each day. And percussion wasn't my only attraction, for I played piano duets with one of the members of the woodwind section who later became Dean of Music at the Washington State University.

At summer's end I returned home to Elkhart and resumed my solo timpani positions in both band and orchestra as well as bell lyra performer in the marching football band. I also continued my piano studies with the best local teacher and played frequently at recitals. I was assigned my first piano concerto; the Grieg *A-Minor Piano Concerto With Orchestra*. But my main attention was still on percussion. I had a xylophone in my bedroom and worked on solos from the George Hamilton Green book as well as those by Harry Bower. In all the regional and national competitions of 1935 I placed first and returned to the National Music Camp for my second year. This time I alternated with Fred Fennell on all percussion parts of importance throughout the summer. We became fast friends for life. He became a famous conductor.

George Way and the Elkhart Community Band

The Elkhart, Indiana, Community Band played weekly summer concerts in the Conn Band Shell behind the C.G. Conn plant in the early 1930s. Since Leedy and Ludwig & Ludwig were both made in the same plant, it was only natural for Leedy's George Way and myself to perform together in the percussion section of this band. We played

Moving Back To The Chicago Area

My father in the meantime had been poorly treated by the C.G. Conn Company in the form of being largely ignored at merchandising meetings and the Ludwig & Ludwig division suffered accordingly. Since Conn had purchased Leedy first and paid cash for it, it became their favorite and thus more money flowed in their direction giving them preference in advertising, engineering, and marketing– all to the detriment of Ludwig. I remember my father coming home from the drum plant in the spring of 1934 telling me his latest device for increased Ludwig sales had not even been considered at a recent merchandising board meeting on the main side– meaning the main plant of the Conn Corporation on the north side of the St. Joseph river in Elkhart. He was deeply discouraged at the enforced decline of Ludwig & Ludwig's reputation and sales position. Little did I know that in the back of his head was a plan to move back to Chicago and start a brand new drum company.

Upon completion of that year's semester in June of 1934, we moved back to the Chicago area, settling in Oak Park, Illinois, directly west of Chicago. Dad transferred to the Chicago office of Ludwig & Ludwig at 1611 N. Lincoln (now Wolcott Avenue). I enrolled in the Oak Park-River Forest High School and commenced summer classes. In addition I enrolled in the American Conservatory of Music in downtown Chicago, taking a full load of advanced piano studies, composition, and arranging.

This was a full schedule but I still found time to job around a little. In the fall I auditioned for the position of timpanist in the Chicago Civic Symphony, the training orchestra for the big orchestra. We played right out of the books of the big orchestra and performed under the direction of the associate music director. We played some heavy stuff so I approached the timpanist of the CSO, Edward M. Metzenger, for lessons and was accepted.

Life was not always easy. I recall one incident which was most embarassing. The conductor was Hans Lange, who was associate conductor under the CSO's Frederick Stock. We were working on Beethovan's *Symphony No. 5*. Maestro patiently explained to all ninety members of our orchestra that he wanted a big retard at a certain number in the score. We went back to the beginning and I played right through the passage in question at full tempo. He stopped the orchestra and glared up at me. I could have crawled into the kettle. He said most caustically, "You have the mind of a bird." That is what I was called for the entire season– bird brain! But it taught me to concentrate even harder on all comments and conversation from the podium and believe me, that never happened again!

High School– Third Year

When the new semester opened in the fall of 1934, I was a member of a brand new student body and slow to make new friends. Oak Park High School was not known for its music program and was far behind most high schools including Elkhart High School. The timpani were a hand tuned pair, 25 and 28-inch, sitting on dinky little folding stands at the height of a midget. They were designed for seated performance, not standing. To perform in my accustomed standing position, I had to tip them up severely. In addition they sounded like tom-toms! I complained to the director and he said there was not money for new instruments in the budget and if I didn't like it the next fellow in line could perform the timpani parts. I wasn't about to give up without a fight so I went directly to the principal, Mr. McDaniels, and explained the problem. He was less than sympathetic. My next step was to check out the sales price of a pair of new Ludwig balanced-action timpani, the same models we had at Interlochen. The price was $350.00, but through my father, we got the price down to $250.00. I took this price back to McDaniels and he secured the

necessary commitment from the board and purchased the new set. I was so proud and really enjoyed them for the rest of my time at this high school. But unfortunately the money was not forthcoming, so I called on the superintendant once a month for payment and he called me once a month for my poor grades! We were gridlocked! Finally, after six months of this nonsense, the board of education came through with the $250.00 and I was off the hook with my dad and the company! Never again did I attempt to sell a school board anything wholesale and I learned my first business lesson. The sale is never complete until you get the money!

European Marimba Tour– 1935

That winter I auditioned for a position in the International Marimba Symphony Orchestra (IMSO) and won a position in the 3rd section as lead player. The leader, Clair Omar Musser, explained that, although I was qualified to play in the 1st section, he needed first chair section leaders with experience in each of the five sections of the orchestra. One hundred players were selected– fifty boys and fifty girls. The marimbas (made specially for this group) were offered at cost to each player's family.... $500.00 each with trunks for transport. Thus started my first European tour.

When I announced my decision to make the trip to my orchestra director (Mr. Embs), he said I would miss a semester of school and this would compromise my education forever. I looked at it as high adventure and an advancement of my musical career.

The IMSO was to travel to England in May to open the festivities in connection with the 25th anniversary of the reign of King George V. Then, we were to cross the channel to France and continue through most of Europe. We practiced mightily three times a week in the Deagan factory on Berteau Avenue in Chicago. (All the members lived in the Chicago area as well as Indiana and Wisconsin.)

Finally on May 1st, we left by special through train for Greenbrier Springs Hotel at Greenbrier, West Virginia. It was there we connected up with the rest of the orchestra, mostly from Pennsylvania which was Mr. Musser's home state. All one hundred marimbas and players dressed in formal attire made a wonderful and most formidable sight and sound. We played there all day every day in the hotel's ballroom, honing our skills and tightening the ensemble sound. It was by far the largest marimba group ever assembled. We played a program of classics that lent themselves to marimba sound and technique.

On the 10th of May we embarked on the liner "Paris" for Southampton, England. During the five day cross-

International Marimba Symphony Orchestra at the Greenbrier Hotel, 1935

Two of the 50 women, aboard the super liner
Ile de France

ing, twenty of us set up our marimbas in the ship's salon and entertained the passengers each night with selections from our repertoire. The ship rolled and so did the King George marimbas. I was one of the few players with a stomach to play every night on the crossing.

The Continent

We arrived off Southampton, England, the sunny morning of May 17th only to find that the ship was not allowed to enter the harbor for docking. It seems that a dispute existed between the British Musician's Union and our New York Local over admittance of the British band of Ray Noble and we were, therefore, held hostage off Southampton. All of our two hundred trunks were up on deck, a lighter was tied alongside; we were on deck with our bags and suitcases, but not allowed to disembark. A meeting was called in the ship's salon by Mr. Musser and he explained the situation. We would proceed to Paris without opening the coronation anniversary ceremonies as planned.

Since it is only a sixty mile voyage across the English Channel to the French ports of LeHavre, we ar-

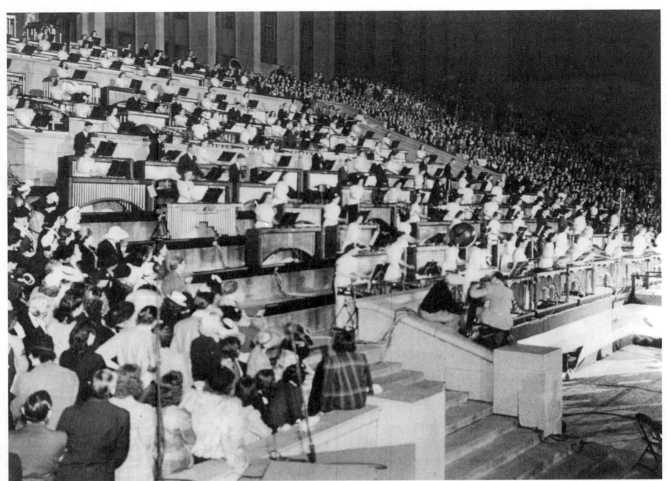

In 1930 Clair Omar Musser, the lone marimba soloist in all of vaudeville, lost his job along with 18,000 other percussionists due to Vitaphone. A Deagan endorser, he convinced Mrs. Ella Deagan to hire him as sales and marketing manager for the J.C. Deagan firm in Chicago. Pictured here is one of his marketing moves; a 100-piece marimba orchestra at the 1934 Chicago Tribune Festival at Soldier Field, playing to a capacity crowd of 100,000!

The International Marimba Symphony Orchestra at Carnegie Hall: This was the final concert in May of 1935; the end of the tour and the end of the orchestra.

rived at dockside at dusk the same day. In two hours we were unloaded and on our way to Paris on the "boat" train. Since the London engagement was canceled, we were ahead of schedule which afforded us sufficient time for sightseeing and believe me, the French capital had plenty of sights for teenagers. Bear in mind this was May 1935; long before transatlantic air travel and so there were few American tourists. We were a rarity–particularly with one hundred very large and heavy King George marimbas in two hundred Taylor-made steamer trunks. Everywhere we went we were questioned by English-speaking French people about why we were there and what life was like in our home country. We felt like ambassadors of good will and determined to play our best. We set the marimbas up in the basement of the concert hall called the Salle Playel which was itself subterranean as a the result of World War I bombardment experiences. Rehearsing in the lowest level was a little uncomfortable and resulted in an awkward setup of the sections. Mr. Musser was not able to attend all the rehearsals so I was asked to conduct them, having had some conducting lessons at Interlochen just three years previously. Nothing compared to our first concert on the grand stage of the Salle Playel dressed in our finest formal attire and flowers flooding the front of the stage.

The program opened with a rousing *Bolero* written especially for us by the Brazilian composer E. Rosales. Next came pieces by Chopin, Franck, Wagner, and Moszkowski. It was a well balanced program with appeal for all audiences. Unfortunately, we were playing for a French audience only and their reaction was rather negative. Our conductor Clair Musser noticed this quickly and decided to depart from the printed program. He called upon our bi-lingual member, Mr. Jack Collins, to address the audience telling them of the changes in the program. The audience found Jack's Frenchy effort touching and from then on we felt a more receptive and relaxed mood from the audience. Some in the audience had walked out! This fact, in addition to the poor attendance to begin with, did not auger well for the rest of the tour.

We packed up everything and left for Brussels, Belgium. I mean we literally packed it up since the French warehouse men went on strike. The Brussels concert went better; our programming made more sense. Our tour plans to enter Germany were forestalled because of a Jewish member, Maggie Hanesack. German officials boarded the train to check all passports just before we crossed the border. They made it clear that Maggie would not be allowed to enter Germany because she was Jewish. As a matter of principal, Mr. Musser re-

fused to leave her behind. So back to Paris we went with our trucks bulging with marimbas and trunks. We set up once more in the basement of the Salle Playel while Mr. Musser pulled out all the public relations stunts in his bag of tricks. That night the hall was nearly full and few left during our more carefully orchestrated program.

Alas.... it was too late. We ran out of money. We didn't have enough to pay our hotel bills plus the boat tickets home. Were it not for the J.C. Deagan company of Chicago I might have grown up French! The genial and most personable Ella Deagan, president of Deagan, wired us $10,000.00 to buy our tickets for the return voyage and clear our hotel bills, releasing our luggage which had been impounded.

Since the orchestra was split between three hotels, runners had to communicate to us that we should grab our luggage, hail taxis– ANY taxis, and head for the North train station. When we arrived, some got on the train and opened windows as we passed our luggage up to friendly hands even when the train was in motion. Fortunately none were left behind.

The last and final concert of the 100-piece International Marimba Symphony Orchestra took place the end of May, 1935, at the venerable Carnegie Hall. It was truly a gala affair. This time the advance publicity went out on time and that filled the hall partially making up the lost money in Europe caused mainly by our dislocated concert tour schedule. If we had been able to open the 25th anniversary celebration of the reign of King George V at London's Covent Garden as planned and if we had not been turned aside by Germany, it is quite possible we would have at least broken even. It remains my personal opinion that the drain of engineering and building those one hundred and one King George marimbas and then destroying the tooling plus the financial loss hurt the solidity of the J.C. Deagan Company. This set in motion the slow but irreversable decline of the Deagan Company. Certainly Jack Deagan was no man to turn it around after World War II, particularly with the loss of their key personnel after the War when Jack refused to hire back his two-man sales force. This resulted in the resignation of Mr. Clair Musser himself, as well as the loss of his key marketing force– Mr F.K. (Pep) Peppler, Robert Viol and engineer Henry Schluter. The short-lived Musser Marimba Company's five-year existence took Jack Deagan's attention away from the business and split whatever marimba and vibe business there was between them. Slowly, slowly, Musser Marimba's new owner Dick Richardson pulled away from Deagan in sales and financial solidity.

We returned home from the IMSO tour with great memories and renewed love of mallet instruments. Returning to Oak Park High School in the fall, I found myself one semester behind and worked like hell to graduate in the spring of 1936 which I did without honors. But my piano training continued at the American Conservatory of Music on Wabash Avenue.

Since the spring of 1936 was free, I traveled with Mr. Musser, his wife, and son with three other players on a ten concert rail trip west to California. Our audiences were railway workers on the Santa Fe railway system who paid our salaries and all expenses to the West Coast. Since there were only five of us (Mrs. Musser did not play) we were expected to play instruments other than just marimba. Mr. Musser conducted we five with the same vigor as the year before leading 100 marimbas in concert! I was expected to perform a piano number between marimba numbers as did other members to fill out the program. The Santa Fe Railway system operated division points for their employees who needed some outside touch with the entertainment world and we supplied it. Again the *Bolero* was the most applauded selection and Ketelby's *In a Monastery Garden* the least appreciated. Wrong programs for the wrong people! Another lesson learned the hard way!

I chose to play a lively little tune– Mousorfsky's *Autumn*. This made little sense, since our listeners were rough-edged section hands more grateful for a touch of the hillbilly or at least country music than what they referred to as highbrow music. None had ever heard of a marimba. Upon completion of this, my only piano recital tour, management of the tour wrote us off as, "Don't hire again!" The general manager, in fact, suggested I find something else to do than play piano. I told him I played drums also. His response was, "Play drums, by all means." I asked, "How do you know I play drums well?" He said, "Kid, I've heard you play piano!" That was the end of my concert pianist dreams.

So it was off to the University of Illinois at Champaign, Illinois, in the heartland of prairie country. Austin A. Harding was the conductor of their remarkable band and I became solo timpanist after auditions that fall. I joined a fraternity since my good friend, Clark Bachman (son of the famous Harold Bachman, leader of WWI Bachman's Million Dollar Band), was also at the U of I where he was first chair in the flute section.

The Illinois band of 120 members was truly a symphonic organization. First of all, Dr. Harding was a very close friend of the "March King" John Philip Sousa, and secondly, the vast library Dr. Harding had augmented with his own transcriptions of symphonic works coupled with the entire Sousa library made it the best in the nation. The John Philip Sousa library had been willed to the university through Dr. Harding's friendship and we were indeed privileged to find original compositions in the master's own hand in our folios!

I really revelled in playing in that band. It broadened me greatly and coming on the heels of my piano fiasco helped restore my self-confidence. Not entirely, however. Although my musical appetite was fulfilled in the band, I found the College of Economics less interesting. My fraternity brothers, including Clark Bachman, tried to help, but my heart wasn't in it.

The next spring (1937) on April 1st my father organized and opened for business his second drum company, the William F. Ludwig Drum Company. That summer I reported for duty in the office and was shocked at how empty it was. Little machinery, and just a handful of employees. Just six or so in the office and a mere two dozen in the factory. There was little in the way of tooling as well. Most, if not all, was used equipment since capital was extremely limited to say the least. My father was bankrolling the entire operation with the sale of his C.G. Conn stock which he had seen erode from one million dollars in 1930 to one hundred thousand in 1937. He had sold Ludwig & Ludwig for $1,000,000.00 in stock and a non-compete clause for five years. Now seven years later it was worth no more than $100,000.00!

He and my mother had debated long and hard over starting up again in the drum business. It was a toss-up whether they would put money into an apartment building in Maywood, one of Chicago's oldest suburbs, live in it and maintain it, or build drums. Thank goodness they chose drums or I might be pumping gas today and even that is drying up due to self-serve pumps now. That is what stared me in the face in 1937!

My first assignment was to sit at a long table to transcribe and write a bell lyra book of fourteen of the most popular Sousa marches for bell lyra, two notes per bar. I finished in August only to discover that the Sousa family forbade any publication without the family's permission and they were not willing to give that. In the meantime, I took my own form of dictation for my father and typed his personal letters. I also typed up the N.A.R.D. (National Association of Rudimental Drummers) quarterly bulletins. Since I was only at the company for the summer, I only put together one bulletin. Little did I know that I would assemble dozens of them through the next forty years!

Since my typing proficiency lent itself to writing up ad copy, I laid out a couple of small ads for such prestigious magazines as *Down Beat* (at that time the musician's Bible of events and happenings in and around

William F. Ludwig Drum Factory, 1936

Artists' embellishments were sometimes used on catalog photographs. The large drum on the corner of the building shown in this photo from the 1941 catalog did not exist in real life!

We used this location to good advantage. We purchased accessories we didn't make yet, such as leg rests for field drums. I guess the Conn Corporation didn't quite know how to handle it's new competitor, us! That was one bill we always paid promptly! Another advantage of being situated near the old company was to take advantage of leading drummers and dealers who would drop in on us after picking up something from Ludwig & Ludwig. The wisdom of my father's location choice slowly dawned on me through the years and I came to realize evermore his genius.

We landed a really big order in the first months of our operation; a complete new set of marching drums for the Commonwealth Edison Utilities Co. championship drum and bugle corps. This corps was made up of Commonwealth Edison employees who were veterans of WWI. The post was incorporated under the rules and regulations of the American Legion as a full Senior Corps for competition in the state and national competitions. The order for twelve snares, four tenors, and six bass drums was not only large but extremely lucrative since it was being built on a cost plus basis through the auspices of my dad's good friend Harold Todd, the drum sergeant of the corps. Who says networking never pays off? This order got us really started; off the chocks as they say in foot racing. Each drum was built by hand of black pearl and chrome plated metal parts. The calf heads were selected by us from American Rawhide's immense stocks and carefully fitted to each drum. No finer set of marching drums were ever built then and now. And how proud we were as they captured both State of Illinois Championships and Nationals as well– best in the nation. The word was gradually spreading– here was a new line of drums in the world!

But alas! A new trouble came at us through legal channels. The Conn Corporation took serious issue with our use of the name "Ludwig" in our title and particularly affixed to the drums themselves. On the advice of

the country). Meanwhile, machinery continued to arrive at the plant daily, as did his experienced department foremen who still lived in the old drum neighborhood.

The Wm. F Ludwig Drum Company was situated just a short three blocks from the old Ludwig & Ludwig office and warehouse and factory.

W.F.L.'s first order in 1937 went to the National Champions; Commonwealth-Edison Co. Post #118, American Legion

6-0, my father, who was in the stands, met me during the second half with the devastating news that he would have to close the W.F.L. Drum Company. I felt a stab in my heart and a great feeling of loss and inadequacy; I was not fulfilling a role of support. My father was carrying the battle alone. When the band returned to Champaign-Urbana, my grades really went to hell. We exchanged letters and they were dismal. Few orders and less cash. The principal of $100,000.00 was fast slipping away. The well was drying up. The name change from Wm. F. Ludwig to W.F.L. Drum Co. was losing trade; we had lost our identity. Conn had won a great victory.

our attorney we agreed to drop our name and change to a new one. We ran through dozens of names; Chicago Drum Company, National Drum Company, World Drum Company, Midwest Drum Company, and finally decided to simply use our initials; WFL Drum Company. This change came in September just as I reluctantly departed for my second year at the University of Illinois.

I returned to Urbana/Champaign in the fall of 1937, rejoining my fraternity mates as well as the University of Illinois Concert Band and the Marching Illini as well. Fall is a golden time in the Midwest. Leaves turning color, a briskness in the air, and, of course, football. The Illinois Band was augmented for marching purposes from 100 to 240 members at home games. Our specialty was playing rather than marching. At every performance Dr. Harding inserted one of his stunning concert arrangements. One, I recall, as especially thrilling, was the concert arrangement of Alfred's *The World Is Waiting For The Sunrise*. The concert band was augmented by the two regimental bands and stretched from goal post to goal post. The crowd of 44,000 fans stood transfixed, and I mean *still*, not a person stirring, as the gigantic clarinet section welled up in the trio, carrying the main theme solo. These concert-field performances made the University of Illinois bands and Austin A. Harding famous around the world. I was proud to be a part of it, even though a small part.

The rest of my academic work didn't fare as well as the band. I should have enrolled in the school of music. In the fall at a football game in Evanston, Illinois, in a game against Northwestern University which we won

Somehow Dad hung on. Mother gave up her meager savings. Anybody who thinks starting a business is easy is in for a rude shock if they try!

On Christmas break I came home and it was very bleak. In addition to one of Chicago's traditional heavy, heavy snow falls, the cold penetrated every bone in your body. W.F.L. Drum Co. was still running, although staggering.

Christmas 1937

I drove to work with Dad daily and he filled me in on the dismal future we faced. Business had been brisk with the introduction of our new twin-spring Speed King pedal in the fall, but drum sales were slack. We had no catalog! The sales manager Sam C. Rowland had been sacked, saving $50.00 per week, but little literature had been generated to tell the trade who and what we were. Christmas Eve (yes, we used to work on Christmas Eve in those days), my father asked me to go to all departments and have everyone come down to the office at 4:30 P.M.

Looking back, I can see they had some premonition that something bad would

The speed king pedal was the most famous pedal the company produced and was the drummers favorite for some fifty years.

happen instead of a Christmas gift. When all sixty of us had assembled, really crowding the tiny office, my father addressed them as follows: "Fellow workers, employees. As you can see we have no orders on the books to fill. Therefore, I am faced with the need to close up shop. We will be closed through these holidays and until Monday, January 10th. If you can find another job, I advise you to take it. Come back if you have not found work on January 10th. Goodbye, and know how hard it is to tell you this on this of all holidays." No one moved at first. My eyes filled with tears. Outside it was snowing again. People were trudging through the snow changing street cars in front of the plant. Slowly, slowly, first one, then another of the bundled employees turned and without a word filed out of the office, down the steps and into the cold snowy night. I climbed the stairs the opposite direction to make my customary closing inspection from the top down. Looking down the stilled rows of benches and machines I was overcome with a tremendous grief and I said aloud "this will *never* happen again. We will continue– we must! And all Christmases from now on *will* be bright and cheery!" And they were!

With this resolve, I returned to the university and handed in my resignation. Gone were fraternity mates, gone the fantastic band days of concerts and marching festivals, gone were studies, homework, and the occasional good times in town. And yes, gone the dance band days on Friday and Saturday night for $4.00 per night.

My Beginning– February 1st, 1938

Since the shutdown of the company on Christmas Eve, some orders for drum sets had come in, notably from two New York music stores; Silver & Horland on Park Row located in south Manhattan and Musical Instrument Exchange on 48th Street. Forty Eighth Street was at that time, and for fifty years thereafter, "musician's row". In just one block between Times Square and Seventh Avenue, there were Al Wolf Drummers Supplies, Manny's Music Company, Selmer's retail store run by Selmer's first president and founder George Bundy, Terminal Music Company, Geodardi's Brass Shop, and a half dozen smaller shops mainly on upper floors. This extremely high concentration of music shops in just one block resulted in intense discounting and set the pace for the rest of the retailers of the world.

The combined Silver & Horland and Musical Instrument Exchange orders amounted to nearly thirty drum sets and on these two orders alone we resumed production on January 10th. All the laid-off employees returned. Not one had found another job. Such was the state of the economy!

The country had just begun to work itself out of the Great Depression when President Franklin D. Roosevelt (at a bridge dedication ceremony) declared our nation closer than ever to war in Europe. That was enough to knock the recovery back down again. Still, with the new orders from New York, we enjoyed a fresh lease on life and I plunged into it with youthful enthusiasm.

Since our first sales manager had been let go, I assumed that role as well as advertising. My salary was pegged at $10.00 per week with $.10 deducted for social security; a grand total of $9.90 per week! I was living at home, which helped. Dating? Forget it! Unless she paid her half. On the other hand, the big amusement park in town, Riverview, had two-cent nights and five dollars went for an entire evening at the park!

In May my first flyer came out. It was announcing our new machine timpani. The pitch changes were accomplished by turning a single handle protruding from the side of the kettle. It was greeted with much enthusiasm by the school trade. The retail price was $250.00 per pair.

First Year Results

By spring, 1938, we had in our hands the financial results of our first nine months of operations: $21,954.00 in sales, with a loss of $14,523.14. This was enough to stand my hair on end. We simply were not selling enough! Our pricing was all right since we simply copied Ludwig & Ludwig's pricing. We knew the Conn company had a huge cost accounting system including platoons of timekeepers watching each operation. Our overhead was already cut to the bone. I was determined to raise our sales through advertising and taking our story on the road. I had the company purchase a gray Plymouth coupe, took out the back partition, filled it with a timpano, tunable tom-tom, and other things like a model of our snare drum and field drum, and headed east.

The Krupa Competition

At every stop I was faced with a life-sized cardboard cutout of Gene Krupa, the then reigning king of drummers. He was depicted standing with a Slingerland Radio King under his right arm and attired in a white suit with white shoes. He was handsome, and very, very successful.

I was told by Krupa that he originally played Ludwig drums purchased from a local retailer, Lyon & Healy on Wabash Avenue in Chicago, but that when he and his father went back after initial successes with the Benny Goodman Band they wanted to charge him the full retail price. Mr. Krupa and Gene then went out to the Ludwig & Ludwig sales office at 1611-27 Lincoln St (now Wolcott Avenue) and were turned down. Their hands were tied. On the corner of Milwaukee Avenue and Damen Avenue there was a restaurant, Halperins, where the Krupas got a telephone book and looked up the available drum suppliers in Chicago and found the Slingerland Drum & Banjo Company. Slingerland had got its start making ukes and banjos. Gene said he didn't want to go there because of the banjos, but his father was determined to take full advantage of his son's new position in the limelight of Chicago's drummers and prevailed. To the Slingerland plant they went.

The Slingerland Drum Company had a most astute sales manager. He was a lively, trim, middle-aged Sam C. Rowland. When the Krupas, father and son, inquired of H.H. Slingerland about a new drum set as a promotional giveaway, Sam Rowland stepped in on Krupa's behalf and convinced "H.H." it would be a wise move to give him what he wanted at no charge. Krupa senior's confidence in Gene was vindicated.

Gene had been listening to African drumming on recordings just beginning to arrive in the United States. He carefully copied that style and requested that Slingerland manufacture a floor tom tom that would be tunable on both top and bottom and stand on his right as he sat at the set. Gene also asked for, and got, a second tunable tom-tom mounted on a holder on the bass drum shell. Thus the four-piece fully tunable set was born with the help of Sam C. Rowland and the sponsorship of the Slingerland Drum Company. This design established itself in the drummer's history for the next forty years and is still offered in most drum catalogs.

In calling on music stores and what drum shops there were at that time (May, 1938) I found it nearly impossible to sell any drums. The dealers asked: "Kid, you got any Gene Krupa drums, or sticks, or wire brushes?" And I would come back with "I have W.F.L. drums and sticks and brushes." I would get an order for sticks and brushes and a few more accessories but seldom anything with a real dollar volume connected to it.

I *did* have the opportunity to tell my story about who we were and who Conn's division Ludwig & Ludwig were, and that there *was* a difference. We were the original Ludwig company in the flesh. Still, I was appalled at the number of orders dealers sent in to Ludwig & Ludwig thinking they were sending them to the W.F.L. Drum Company.

In Cleveland I met an old friend of my father, Henderson N. White; founder and president of the H.N. White Band Instrument Company which was second in size only to the giant C.G. Conn band instrument company. The White Company operated a retail store on the factory premises at 5225 Superior Avenue. (It has now been replaced by an apartment complex.)

Finally arriving in New York City, I hurried to Musical Instrument Exchange and it's genial owner Kelly Goodman. This was followed by calls over the next week to all of the drum dealers in New York City including the venerable and one-time savior of the W.F.L. Drum Co., Herbie Horland and Harry Silver of Silver and Horland at 110 Park Row in the famed Bowery.

New York City is overwhelming and the pace is hectic. In addition to my daytime calls I visited 52nd Street, known then as night club row. My days and nights were filled with drums, orders, and continuous contact work so vital to turning a profit for the company in 1938. (Not to mention just staying in business.) On April 1st we celebrated our first anniversary. That first year had been a hectic one, getting started anew. Three times we had nearly packed it in and closed up shop!

The date of April 1st is one of the most important days in my life to this day. In addition to our anniversary, it marked a great challenge answered and defeated. It happened this way: Slingerland's sales manager Sam C. Rowland overheard Henry Heanon Slingerland dictating a letter to H.N. White of the White Band Instrument Company of Cleveland on the occasion of our opening of W.F.L. Drum Co. on April 1st, 1937. Rowland was so incensed by it that he passed it on to us when he quit Slingerland and came over to our side. Slingerland had written to Mr. White: "Well, I see in the news that Bill Ludwig has started a new drum company, and on April Fool's day at that. Well, there is no fool like an old fool.He won't last a year!" This challenge became our rallying cry. We would last a year and a day to show our enemy he was wrong with his prophecy! And it came to pass that I could send my father the first of many, many telegrams from the road congratulating him on each anniversary in business, with more to come.

With each dealer call I made a complete report which included notes about his inventory and the type of customers he catered to: jazz, professional, and/or school trade. These reports accumulated into quite a useful treasure of sales information, the first we had. In this task my rapid-touch typing helped tremendously. I carried a portable typewriter to my hotel room each night and made out the most complete record of dealer calls I could think of so that when I got back I could follow up.

One extremely important drum shop was the Bill Mather Drum Shop at 314 West 46th Street. It was located in the basement but what a treasure trove of new Slingerland drums and acessories it was. Bill Mather was a jolly Englishman with a talent for handling tools and machinery. He was important not for his sales volume but for his particular talent of customizing the great name drummers' sets. He was the first to adorn drums with shell-mount fixtures which he had specially made by Barney Wahlburg in Worcester, Massachesetts. Slingerland had developed a cozy relationship with Bill Mather, ensuring that drum deals with the big time drummers would go through Slingerland's hands. Mather would alter the hoop-mounted holders with Wahlburg & Auge shell-mount holders. This was a revolutionary innovation back then when all the other holders were mounted on bass drum hoops.

Making the Name Drummer Scene

On this, my first trip to New York City, I soon learned from Bill Mather that it would take a considerable extra investment "under the table" as they say, to break into the "name" drummer business. Gene Krupa at the time was the reigning king of the drums with the fabulous Benny Goodman orchestra and quartet featuring Lionel Hampton on the vibes.

I hung around Mather's Drum Shop the better part of two weeks trying my best to break into this alliance but to no avail. Finally I left for New England and came across the one bright spot of the whole tour. In Hartford there was a man named Adolph B. Cardello running a house full of drums! Yes, literally a house filled on every floor and in every window (and in the summertime on the porch) with drum sets. Cardello was a drummer and operated a complete drum studio featuring a full Gene Krupa set, Gene's new book written by the famous Henry Adler, and a phonograph with the Krupa record *Sing, Sing, Sing* on the turntable. He taught on the drum set and beginning students were introduced to drum playing on a full set. He had dozens of students beating a path to his door, and of course each one was exposed to all those drum sets on display!

After looking over the other dealer in Hartford–Pearlmutters Music, I decided to give in to Cardello's request for an exclusive in Hartford, Connecticut. This was a very dangerous move and not recommended because I would be tying up W.F.L. with no assurance that the dealer, Cardello, would respond in kind by having no other line in his store (house) but mine. But Adolph Cardello was a terrific salesman and convinced me that this was the wise way for us to go. In return he would give me a large order to start and send more in over time. The Pearlmutters complained, especially since Cardello's was a house and we were not to sell retail to people in their houses. But the sincerity of Adolph's business plan plus all those outfits on display lighted day and night plus his one hundred pupils plus my failure to get drum orders so far convinced me this was the way to go. It's very lonely there on the road and decision making isn't easy.

Once the deal was made, exclusive for exclusive (we would sell no other and he would buy no other), he invited me into his house and I checked out of the local hotel. (I say hotel because in those days there were no motels! They hadn't been thought of yet.) Adolph's wife Leora was a terrific cook and I fell in love with Italian food for life!

The arrangement with Cardello lasted six years and led to a close personal relationship between our families. The Cardellos would stay in our house when visiting the music trade shows in Chicago. He sold a heck of a lot of W.F.L. drums!

L-R Wm. F. Ludwig Sr., Wm. F. Ludwig II, Adolph B. Cardello

The Ludwig family made about a dozen of these monsters– six feet in diameter! None were profitable, but it got us some publicity.

The author helping endorser Ray Bauduc into a drum "suit", 1938.

In Boston I looked up Avedis Zildjian in Quincy. This helped insure us an unbroken supply of Zildjian cymbals so important in the beginning. The Zildjians sold their cymbals through wholesalers like the drum companies and a few select music stores. Avedis was really a rugged individualist. One of his longtime employees said Avedis would pick up mail at the post office every morning and open it at his desk. At his elbow was a list of the past-due accounts. Every one of the fresh orders who were on his past-due list was chucked into the waste basket. At the end of the day one of his sons would go through the basket and retrieve those orders and enter them!

In Maine, Portland is the big city. The dealer there (Eastern Music Supply) let me haul all my samples up to his second floor office and they bought only six pair of sticks! When I tried desperately to sell him at least a snare drum or outfit (for he had none in stock or on display) he responded with , "Young fella, do you know how many trees there are in the state of Maine?" Answer: millions. "And how many people live in this state?" About 700,000. He continued, "Now if you think I can sell a snare drum of yours to each of those trees, I'll take a sample from you. If not.... forget it!" I forgot it.

The Evolution of a Plan– Strike Where Slingerland Ain't

I turned West as summer drew to an end and slowly a plan began forming in my mind. Since Slingerland, with his Gene Krupa connection, and Bill Mather monopolized the drum set business, we should concentrate our efforts where he is weak. The school market jumped out in my mind loud and clear. Slingerland had field drums and all sorts of marching bass drums in his big 96-page catalog but they were not pushing this segment of the drum business. Also they were not advertising in the school magazines– especially the state papers. I hatched a plan on my return trip west to concentrate all of our efforts in the school market without giving up the outfit market.

We had Ray Bauduc, the king of Dixieland drumming, as our star but this field was limited and greatly overshadowed by the monolithic Swing Era. Still, Ray Bauduc with the Bob Crosby Band (brother of Bing Crosby) was all we had. Ray was a real sweetheart of a guy with a real knack of mechanical things so he was able to explicitly state his drum needs. Foremost of these was the snare drum which had to be seven inches deep and equipped with wood hoops for a deep, penetrating rim shot sound quite different than the metal hoop rim shot sound. His color was black pearl. We came out with a new self-aligning die-cast lug for him and dubbed it the Ray Bauduc model.

In pursuit of my plan I created quarter-page field drum and concert drum ads for the state educator magazines. These included coupons which enabled me to start accumulating a mailing list of music educators who would receive our first W.F.L. catalog if and when it came out. Another educator magazine I used regularly was *The Instrumentalist* which is still in publication today. Also *The School Musician* which is not.Returning from my first sales trip in the East, I found the business running rather smoothly due to a small but steady increase in orders. Some of my calls made on my ten week trip east were starting to pay off although confusion still existed between our company– W.F.L. Drum Co. and C.G. Conn's division Ludwig & Ludwig. I had to make regular weekly walks to the Ludwig & Ludwig office three blocks away to deliver some of their mail missent to us and vice versa. It was embarassing to say the least, especially having to rely on "them" for parts and accessories such as leg rests for field drums, slings for field drums, and other items we did not carry or make.

Financial Results For The Year 1938–

The outside accountant down the street from us on North Avenue turned in the results of this, our second, year and first full twelve months of operation and it was much better than 1937's first nine months. Sales were $89,463.02 leaving a net profit before taxes of $604.00. Small as it was, it was a profit! We were out of operating in the red but just barely. It was a good time to hit my father for a raise and I got it. My salary "jumped" from $10.00 per week to $15.00 per week with .15 withheld for social security for a net total of $14.85 per week which stayed at that rate for the next two years. Members of the family who worked for the family business were expected to sacrifice! Any readers of these words in a family business will recognize this ancient truth.

The band instrument business in which we were involved really heated up in the fall of each year with school reopenings. It was a time of field drum demand for the football bands taking to the gridiron. The school percussion business is seasonal. The school boards receive their allocation of funds in the spring, payable in the fall. All of the orders were therefore placed in the fall and the strain was terrific to get the drums out in time for the kickoff of the football season. There were no vacations or time off in the fall! Everyone was locked in to their jobs until Thanksgiving. We supplied drums in colors of the customer's choice and this meant every color of the rainbow and then some. Friday nights and Saturdays became crisis times in meeting order expectations. Some orders arrived in time for the last game of the season and of course this would never do. Drums (especially bass drums) are bulky, and since we had limited space, it was impossible to build up an inventory in anticipation of the busy fall season. We used some temporary plans such as renting tractor trailer trucks parked out in back, but this added to our production costs The long term solution was to expand to the north of our main building and this we proceeded to do by buying the house next to our main building— 1732 N. Damen Avenue. We moved in in the spring of 1940 and added a large warehouse in the back yard.

In 1939 we published our first true catalog. I say true because we had been building sales volume by designing and printing flyers. In addition, our office staff was enlarged through

the addition of some of the experienced people from our competitors. This was easier said than done since the cost of living in the Chicago area is always higher than

Ray Bauduc, 1941. Backing the big Bob Crosby Band with his blue and white marine pearl W.F.L. drum set.

In the summers of 1939 and 1940, the Bob Crosby Band played at the Blackhawk Restaurant in the heart of Chicago's loop. On Sundays they attracted large crowds of teenagers from the northern suburbs, especially Winnetka. For them, Ray Bauduc had us design a very special black pearl "Bob Cat" outfit shown here. Sizes were: 4x10 tom, 8x12 tom, and 14x16 floor tom. The bass was 12x22 and the snare (with wood hoops) was 7x14 for a "zoonk" sound on rim shots. The author is seated on the far left, busting with pride!

Cecil Strupe, Chief Engineer, WFL Drum. Co.

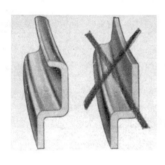

rural areas and this meant we paid higher salaries. The salaries were attractive to new employees, but they had to consider not only the higher cost of living, but also moving expenses. Moving expenses were sometimes considerable, such as when Mr. Strupe moved from Indianapolis to Chicago. Cecil Strupe was one of the first to come our way and was the most brilliant engineer of the day. Strupe had been chief engineer at the Leedy Drum Co. in Indianapolis and later L&S Drum Co. in which he was a partner with Hollis Leedy, one of Mr. U.G. Leedy's sons.

One of the most significant inventions from Mr. Strupe's great mind was the triple-flanged metal hoop. I had been complaining to Cecil about chewed-up drum sticks due to double-flanged hoops. Using pliers, he produced a third flange by bendng outwards the top of the hoop, presenting the sticks with a rounded edge and minimizing cutting of the shoulder of the stick. We immediately tooled up for full scale production and I prepared illustrations and ad copy for the new triple-flanged hoop models. This was a smash hit and sales leaped forward by 40%! Next in line was the accomplishment of a smoother snare thowoff. Throughout 1940, 1941, and half of 1942, Mr.Strupe turned out dozens of drum improvements, some of which are still in use today, over sixty years later. In time, all drums were supplied with triple-flanged hoops.

A Beefed Up Sales Staff

Another area that needed serious attention was the office and sales staff. Orders from dealers were to be properly handled and entered into the production process. Sales materials had to be written and published. In that regard we were fortunate, for the sales manager of our competitor, Fred W. Miller of Ludwig & Ludwig, applied for a position with us. Fred W. Miller had worked for my father in the 1920s and brought to us over twenty years of experience. I literally learned the marketing business at his knees! Palmer C. Laycock was a sales correspondant, formerly with the Leedy Company. Laycock answered all mail communi-

Fred W. Miller

cations through his remarkable ability to touch type without the need of a secretary taking shorthand.

One of the most important departments in any business is the returned goods department. This is the department which is the most difficult to staff. Frequently customers receiving the wrong size drum or wrong color would just box the item up and send it back. Most did not send us a separate letter advising us of this action with the result that their returned items laid in the returned goods section of the plant for a very long time. Finally someone would randomly open the package and find a note inside with instructions as to the desires of the customer. Does he want a replacement? Repair? Order cancellation? If not attended to quickly, confusion results and continued billing for the item irritates the customer no end. Fred Miller showed me how to develop and keep a returned goods file and to open all packages within three days from receipt of same.

One of the great benefits of this experience is that you find out the weaknesses in your product line. And your quality as well! Returned products often point an accusing finger at the company's product line and having one of the owners (me) handle this taught many lessons at an early stage in my development as an all-around percussion technician.

Ask the owner of a business what he thinks of his returned goods department and he'll tell you it is really a pain and no one wants to be involved with it if they can avoid it. But management must resist the temptation to put the lowest paid or most recent hire to work as the manager of return goods. This is a high quality and good will position. I remember the time we got an order from a Portland, Oregon, dealer for a blue bass drum for the local school and on the very same day an order for a white bass drum from a dealer in Portland, Maine. You guessed it! The orders went into the system reversed and neither dealer was happy when blue went east and white went west. Both bass drums were shipped back, of course, through the returned goods department.

The Endorsee Scene

My first endorsee for our drums was Ray Bauduc with the famous Bob Crosby Band. Ray was one of the acknowledged Dixieland favorites of the 1930s and '40s. He was lined up by our first sales manager, Sam Rowland. One of the first projects was to build a special bird's eye maple drum set to Ray's specifications. The second was to corroborate on a drum book carrying the name of Ray Bauduc on its cover but largely assembled and written by Sam Rowland.

The Crosby band played each summer in the old Blackhawk Restaurant on Wabash Avenue in Chicago and that gave me plenty of time to work with him in the design of his very special "Bob Cat Outfit" comprising five drums in black pearl all nearly half size compared to a normal set. This was pulled out on the dance floor

three times a night for special performances with the "Bob Cats"– a five-piece combo made up to perform during floor shows. The restaurant served excellent full-course dinners as well as cocktails and the audience was invited to sit around the drum set during every performance. A special rubber treaded mat was used to move the set on and off the floor, there being no stairs to contend with.

Sunday afternoons were advertised as special days and appealed to the teenage kids and an especially large contingent always showed up from a north side suburb called Winnetka. In honor of these teenagers, Ray corroborated with bass player Bobby Haggart in a special number entitled "Big Noise From Winnetka". This arrangment involved all players until the bridge where Ray would switch from the snare drum to the string bass strings. He played the strings rhythmically with his sticks and whistled the melody while Haggard fingered the melody. The sticks striking the strings was such a novelty that the kids went wild with joy and Ray had many encores to play at almost every performance.

The Crosby arrangements dug deeply into the heritage of New Orleans dixieland styles and harmony. The rhythm was mainly two beats per measure with a laid back style. It wasn't truly "swing" but awfully close to it.

I worked hard at lining up other "name" drummers. I would work all day at the plant including Saturdays and go home for dinner. Then freshen up and drive downtown to the Loop to make my artist calls. In the final years of that decade– 1938, 1939, 1941 and 1942, I lined up Lionel Hampton, Frankie Carlson with the Woody Herman Band, and George Wettling with the famous Paul Whiteman organization.

Smokin' Clubs and Drums

In those days of the '30s and '40s everybody smoked cigarettes. A friendly form of greeting was to offer someone a cigarette, light up, and chat. Therefore the clubs were always full of smoke to the extent the smoke hung in layers from floor to ceiling. I had been smoking Philip Morris "ciggies" since my high school days, so I had no problem falling in line.

Calling on a drummer entailed much smoking and drinking while awaiting the drummer to come visit

Important visitors to the assembly department in 1939: (l-r) the author, Jo Jones (known for his brush work), tennis star Gene Mako, and local drummer Marty Greenburg

beween sets. It was in this environment that I worked the "night shift" as I called it, calling on the "trade" night after night in Chicago's glittering night clubs and fine restaurants. Some were really gaudy, featuring complete floor shows for the diners three times a night. These places were The Palmer House, Sherman House Panther Room (named after the decor of the furniture and walls in a tiger skin motif), and the Chez Parree. The Chez Parree was the most famous of them all, complete with Can-Can chorus girls. Other places were more like today's jazz clubs offering only food, liquor, and good jazz music. I made them all– night after night after night and working day after day at the factory. Sundays were my days of recuperation; sleeping late and getting rid of the red eyes. It's tough to be a milkman and bartender at the same time!

Financial Results in 1939–1941

In 1939 we sold $170,000.00 worth of drums and accessories with a net profit of $4,248.09. 1940's sales were $221,831.35 with net profit of $6,730.86, and 1941 saw sales of $324,193.34 and a net profit of $35,672.65. We were growing in strength and, more importantly, profitability due to a careful watch of all expenses. This afforded us an improvement in our standard of living, as we purchased a house in the beautiful Chicago suburb of River Forest We no longer had the fear of failure and we were getting to be a power in the education field. My father and I complimented each other rather nicely in alternating drum clinics throughout the country, sometimes appearing on programs together. My technique was the exact mirror image of his; teacher and pupil. He had a roll like peas rolling down a tin roof that I never accomplished. We were very much like a vaudeville act of old. I remember one occasion at the

The Ludwig home in River Forest, Illinois

Midwest Band Clinic in the grand ballroom of the Sherman House Hotel when Dad was speaking and in the middle of an explanation on roll technique, he was seized by a coughing fit. Without hesitation, I stood up and finished the sentence and ran down the long roll as I had been taught years before. Thank God for those years of hard work on the practice pad he forced on me!

Each year at Christmas I privately celebrated my promise of 1937– "this will never happen again". I was able to wish a Merry Christmas to each employee and give each a gift. One year it was cartons of cigarettes; the next, individual wine bottles, and in 1940, food for their tables. I recall so vividly that Christmas Eve at the plant. I had gone through the employees list very carefully for their preferences– a frozen ham or turkey. When the time came, I was ready with the presentation of their choice. When all had left the office to step into the snow and ice of a typical Chicago Christmas, one of them returned. I was relaxing in my office swivel chair when the door opened and a very angry Tony Maturo, our wood shop foreman, burst through the door and with one mighty heave, flung his ham across the office, landing first on a desk, then bouncing off the floor and ricocheting off of desk and chair legs until finally coming to a spinning stop in front of me. Tony literally hissed out, "I wanted a turkey!" He left and for one of the few times in my life I was truly speechless. My, how a little prosperity can change things! That was the last time I ever gave food, liquor, or cigarettes as gifts. For the rest of my life I relied on checks– much, much simpler and no rejects!

The Battle of The Ads

One drummer I really wanted in my stable of stars was Buddy Schutz with the Jimmy Dorsey Orchestra. Buddy was a straight-out hard-driving swing drummer and we were still weak in that department. I convinced him after many visits and hanging out backstage (a $5.00 bill got me in every time) and innumerable cups of coffee between shows at the State-Lake Theater, that I could do a better advertising job for him than H.H. Slingerland. I explained to him that Slingerland would always spend the bulk of their advertising budget on Krupa and all the rest of the many drummers would have to be satisfied with what was left. We, on the other hand, had but half a dozen swingers and Ray Bauduc in the Dixieland classification. I must have done a better job of convincing Buddy because backstage he looked up Mr. Slingerland's home phone number and told him at home that he was switching his allegiance to W.F.L.! I was stunned at this rather

28

cold and very abrupt action but stood by helplessly at this abrupt move. "Not good," I thought. I had caused one of Slingerland's stars to enrage H.H. and so the next two issues of *Down Beat* magazine carried quarter-page ads of Buddy Schutz with Dorsey. This undercut the impact of my ads which appeared in the following issues of *Down Beat* magazine.

The net result of my actions was that I got a good drummer but an avalanche of Slingerland ads in the following months– some featuring some of my stars taken from me. Lesson: let your competition have time to clear his ad schedules before you run one of his defector's ads. Do it in a gentler, cleaner fashion and you'll avoid the knife edge of revenge.

One Last Shot at Krupa

The Krupa-Slingerland partnership raged on with Krupa's resignation from the Benny Goodman Orchestra to form his own band. Only one other time in all musical history had there been a band with a drummer as its leader and that was the Ben Pollack organization

Edward M. Metzenger, Timpanist, Chicago Symphony Orchestra

of the 1920s. In that band Pollack played and led the band from a drum set out in front. Now, twelve years later, Gene Krupa followed suit but led the band from the normal drummer's position to the left of center. Slingerland constructed very clever music stands fronted with marine pearl and inlaid with Gene's initials in black pearl. In addition, an 8x12 rack tom was mounted to the player's left on each one of the music stands. At a particular point in Krupa's long featured drum solo, the band picked up sticks and joined in by ranks: saxes first, trombones next, and trumpets last. It was a truly dramatic effect and brought down the house each time it was played.

The Krupa management and booking agency booked his band into leading American theaters and it was a smash hit. How I suffered! More than ever the drum customers were flocking to Slingerland-Krupa products.

In the years after my first road trip East, I had increasingly turned my attention to the West; the Southwest to be more specific. Here was the most fertile field to sell school drums and, of course, our timpani. However, the tremendous victories Slingerland was enjoying could not help but lure me on into one last supreme effort in having Gene play W.F.L. drums.

Back to New York I went, in 1940 I think it was, to a trade show at the famed New Yorker Hotel where we displayed our line. Gene and his hugely successful band were playing out on Long Island at a ballroom known as the Glen Island Casino. I went there and contacted his manager, Pat McGurn. He said, "Let's go out to the car and talk." In his Cadillac, he made an offer to turn Gene Krupa over to W.F.L. for $35,000.00 cash. He said he controlled Gene and he would play whatever drums he told him to. He said there had been many other drum companies approaching him, but he would give me first chance.

I thanked him and told him I would think it over and let him know our decision. I called my Dad and he turned the offer down immediately. The reader should consider that $35,000.00 in 1940 would be the equivalent of at least $210,000.00 in today's economy. The highest priced drum in our catalog had a retail price of $65.00. How many would have to be sold with a net profit of $5.00 per drum? In other words, how long would it take for us to earn a return on our investment? I reluctantly turned it down.

History proved that this was a good move because in only two years, Pearl Harbor was attacked by the Japanese Imperial Government and drum production was all but eliminated.

Good Bye Gene– Good Bye Drum Set Sales

Even though the 1940 blue cover W.F.L. catalog featured Ray Bauduc and his Dixieland Outfit, the contents of this catalog were heavily weighted towards school items following my then two and a half year old plan.

Following "The Plan", I concentrated on school and drum corps sales. I launched a great many drum clinics by running down the more important rudiments, and followed up with current cadences. Timpani technique was my forte for I was still a student of the Chicago Symphony's timpanist, Edward Metzenger. Ed would come out to the plant Saturdays and since we had cut back in the shop to the forty hour week, we had the plant all to ourselves. I would have a set of timps pulled out of production all tuned up and ready to go.

One of his solid tips was never to cross stick if you can possibly avoid it. The danger in cross sticking is hooking a stick and sending it flying off into a distant brass or fiddle section. Another tip was to start every roll with a single stroke to get the head vibrating and establish the entrance and then follow up with the same hand thus RRLRLR, etc. When attacking a fortissimo roll alternately, the timpanist presents a good solid flam which is not what is written in the part.

After an hour's lesson, we would lock up the plant and walk a block down Damen Avenue to the corner saloon for a beer and a shot with polish sausage sandwiches. We were in the middle of the largest concentration of Polish people outside of Warsaw. And the polish sausage was so good after a hefty lesson! The proprietor was a big, beefy Russian immigrant, Boris, who had escaped from the old Soviet Union by literally walking out of the country into Poland and sneaking into America. People weren't too inquisitive in those days.

I feel at this point I should explain what a "shot and beer" consisted of at corner saloons around the W.F.L.factory. You order a schooner of beer and a shot of whiskey. Then drop the shot glass and all and let it settle to the bottom. As you sip your beer, the whiskey ascends to the top and your body slowly experiences the most glorious warming you can ever experience. A couple of these and Ed Metzinger would loosen up for some really inside stories about symphony orchestra work. For instance, there are many cliques within the organization. And there are some members who have never talked with certain other members, sometimes out of jealousy. Ed often talked about what the members thought of various guest conductors. One conductor conducted without the score. A soloist in the brass section placed his horn to his lips two measures before his entrance. When the scoreless conductor saw the horn come up, he cued the soloist. The brass player shook his head no, holding up two fingers to indicate there were two more measures before his entrance. That conductor felt cut down!

After concerts, "Metz" and I would stop off at the corner saloon on Monroe Street for his specialty "post-concert relaxation"– a glass of sherry wine with a raw egg yolk in it! The first of the viagra treatments.

Clinic Tours

So with this great background, I took to the road in earnest, seeking out the shows and exhibitions where I could wiggle onto the program. One such prime spot was a little town in central Oklahoma named Enid where a music festival of thousands assembled every May to compete in performance as well as marching. This event covered four days in May. I was able to get on the program every year and thus tell my W.F.L. story. In such manner business is obtained and thus built up through the years. But not all goes as planned! At one of these festivals in 1940, I was given a prime spot for a lecture. It was 8:00 P.M. following a banquet. I was very proud to have such a prestigious audience of band directors as well as college students. The main director of the evening, Austin A. Harding, (my old conductor at the University of Illinois), got up at the dinner's conclusion and announced that the directors were leaving and excusing themselves from my clinic because "they had heard all this before"! I was crushed. I mean really smashed and deflated. Those who were left retired to the auditorium and I began my one and a half hour clinic on a downbeat note since my audience was pitifully small.

But sometimes good things spring from devastation. I had brought with me from Chicago one of our new pedal tuned timpany. At the end of the performance part, I stated that this new model of ours was very easy to separate bowl from stand and reset up again. It came apart easily as planned but, alas, I spoke too soon about putting it back together again. I just couldn't, so finally, after what had to be the most embarassing ten minutes of my life, I left it apart and concluded the lecture. After everyone left, I packed up with a new lesson learned on the speaking circuit. *Never oversell your product!* Take it apart, yes, but don't attempt a re-assembly in front of your audience. That lesson learned early stood me in good stead for the rest of my business life!

Shell Construction in the 30s and 40s

In the beginning, W.F.L. drums were produced with three-ply shells reinforced with two maple glue rings. Two outer panels of mahogany long grained were laid up with one inner panel of short cross grained poplar. This cross-grained layup produced a very lightweight yet sturdy shell. The inner glue rings acted as reinforcements and also held the true round circumference. Occasionally maple veneer would be added on the outside layer replacing mahogany because the maple grain is tighter and finishes up smoother. We also introduced a line of birds-eye maple exteriors which finished up producing a gleaming finish. These shells were , of course, more expensive. Birdseye finishes were our most appealing finish.

Then the shell was scarfed at each end to produce a bearing edge. Some shells were sanded carefully to accept a covered plastic sheet which was available in a multitude of finishes. These lightweight shells were a trademark of the W.F.L. line and followed the tradition of my father to produce lightweight yet strong drums and accessories. We always had the drummer in mind packing, carrying, and setting up his equipment. These wonderful, durable shells plus our exclusive triple flanged metal hoops made for a very competitive drum line which gradually overcame all competition and restored our former claim as "standard of the world". Together with our patented twin strainer design this helped establish a competitive edge which was hard to beat.

The W.F.L. Plant in 1941– The Last Full Year of Production Before World War II

Each of the years 1937–1941 had shown a healthy slow but steady volume increase in both units and dollars. In the new 1941 catalog factory pictures

The original wood shop in 1938 covered 8,000 square feet, with another 5,000 square feet in the basement. Laminated woods were carefully blended to produce the best sounds. Then they were reinforced with solid maple inner reinforcement bands to provide lasting strength and durability. Only the finest skilled artisans with many years of experience are allowed to hand finish all wood shells and hoops. The steam bending machines could turn out 200 shells per day.

The machine shop in the Ludwig (WFL) factory as it appeared in 1940. All metal stands and parts were machined to close tolerances providing a perfect interlocking fit. In the left lower corner appears a section of the famous Ludwig pedal line. The photographer taking these factory pictures complained at the lack of workers in each picture. I then brought employees from other floors and posed them in order to fill out the work force!

The (calfskin) head-tucking table

appeared: The building was a three story with full basement stone and brick construction consisting of quarry stones dating from the year 1900.

It was a corner building on the north side of Wabansia Ave, but fronting for fifty feet on Damen Avenue. Street car tracks ran up and down Damen Av-

enue and the elevated trains were just three blocks to the south making location easy for many of the neighborhood employees. With full all-day sunlight on all floors it was a cheery building and one I always thought worth the $18,000.00 purchase price in 1936. By 1940 all the machinery was in place and even modernization was beginning through the buying skills of my father and our wonderful genius chief engineer Mr. Cecil H. Strupe. We made as much as we needed in this plant and gradually eliminated our dependence on outside sources. When you make it yourself you control everything– the volume, inventory, quality, price, and improvements. This was the old world philosophy of my father and his brother Theobald.

All our special machinery such as the steam bending machines with 10 to 1 reduction gears were designed by Mr. Strupe and built in our plant. We made our own stick dipping tanks which were marvels in applying a

The third floor final assembly department of the Ludwig complex as it looked in 1940. Lacquered multicolored shells were sold in that decade as well as wrapped shells. Only the finest hand-crafted drums reached the shipping room for the last production stage of packing and shipping. The factory superintendant and department manager are seen in the center of this picture going over every detail of a finished shell.

streak-proof finish lacquer to our sticks and beaters. Our rip saws, band saws, most dies, clamps, and jigs were built internally. Therefore, they were better than the competition. The aim was to increase productivity to hold down costs.

We were so successful, in fact, that by the end of 1940 we had attracted the attention of the Piano and Musical Instruments Workers Union AFL and were organized. This Union also had seven other plants in its group so we felt fairly comfortable being in such prestigious company– Kimball Piano Company, Gulbranson Piano Company, P.A. Starck Piano Company, Kay Guitars and Harmony Guitars and so on. But not Slingerland. We heard through the grapevine that H.H. Slinglerland himself bodily threw organizers out of his plant and took the $4,000.00 government fine readily. He wasn't about to sit down with anyone in the matter of wages and terms of employment in his factory!

A W.F.L. Factory Tour In 1940

We start with the basement, of course. This was a room fifty feet by a hundred feet– 5,000 square feet.Of course, it always flooded in a heavy spring or summer rain which wasn't all bad because it made us move everything to dry out and in so doing we discovered wood that had been lying around much too long for its own good. The coal-fed furnace was in the rear– yes, I said coal! This meant that every Sunday afternoon I would have to go into town, open up to feed the fire and bank it so that Monday mornings were reasonably warm in the winter time. When the four of us as a family would go downtown to take in a show at the Chicago Theatre, it was always followed by a stop by the plant on Damen Avenue to shovel coal as a father and son team while mother and sister waited in the car!

Some Monday mornings the entire work force would

be lined up after punching in, warming themselves and none of the foremen would dare move them out until the knocking in the pipe announced that the heat was at last coming through. Of course, this cost us some down time but it couldn't be helped until in the middle of 1942. We felt we could afford converting that old boiler to oil fuel with an automatic thermostat!

Twice a month, a flat bed lumber truck would dump 4,000 board feet of fine hard maple long planks on the grass strip alongside the sidewalk. The basement crew would come up with winter clothing and passed each individual piece through the lower basement windows to the basement inside crew who stacked the maple in neat racks alongside the rip saw. This saw would cut the maple boards into counterhoop widths. From here they were fed into a planer which quickly, and above all, accurately smoothed top and bottom of the strips. From here the strips were passed into the angler which planed the tips so that when bending no part of the maple hoop would be fatter than any other part. It was a tight space, that room, and noisy, but always very busy. And the odor! That lovely virgin wood odor.– I tell you it was heavenly.

Next, the office. Not very large, but efficient. Orders came in and were filled promptly. Here is where I spent almost all my time when not on the road or setting up displays at conventions like the annual National Association of Music Merchants trade show every summer. This was our biggest show and alternated between the Palmer House in Chicago and the Hotel New Yorker in odd years. A lot of planning went into these shows and still does. Decisions have to be made concerning what to display; then it had to be built, assembled, and shipped in time to be set up at the hotel.

Behind the office were the all-important bending machines continuously revolving slowly all day long every day. The speed of these machines determined just how many drum shells would be produced in a day. We started with one bending machine but by 1941 we had two. We could roll 200 shells per day!

The W.F.L. office assembled for a Christmas, 1941, portrait. There were now 14 members. Wm. F. Ludwig Sr. is seated in the center with son Bill II, sixth from right, and Bettie Ludwig, second from right.

The woodshop was perhaps the noisiest department in the whole operation and I am sure contributed to my hard of hearing problems years later. The noisiest by far was the single Nash stick lathe in the back of the room. Each hickory dowel was spun at 2400 revolutions per minute and when the cutting circular blade was engaged to form the drum stick, it made a howling scream. Since a good deal of sawdust was in the air at all times, the cyclone air ventilation system had to remove the dust and scrap from each ma-

The author and F.K. (Pep) Peppler on the road to the Pacific Coast from South to North and back. Pep served in World War II as an Artillery Officer in the Italian campaign of 1943-44 and joined me full time after his service to his country.

chine, blow it up to the roof where it circulated and then dropped into the basement sawdust vault which had to be emptied daily. I mention this because all the hand labor was used to not only run these operations but clean the plant daily.

The second floor was devoted to the machine shop which contained Mr. Strupe's engineering office with a draftsman and purchasing officer. Here were located lathes, screw machines, and, of course, punch presses that rocked the ceiling below. I recall my one and only visit to the Slingerland office on an industry problem and sitting in Mr. Slingerland's office. The punch presses were located directly above his desk and what a racket he had to endure!

Final Assembly

Everything now had to arrive on the third and final floor and fit properly. Here the shells and hoops were sprayed and the giant spray booth was mounted on a newly laid thick concrete floor as a fire prevention measure. The spraying operation in any drum plant is by far the most dangerous because of the volatility of the materials lying about. The wood shells were mounted on circular tables and a hand-held spray gun then applied the desired finish. When dry, the shells entered the drilling department for holes to be punched to receive the hardware. The assembly bench on this floor stretched almost the entire length of the building and faced south, thus, constantly bathed in sunlight. This is so important in achieving the desired quality. Then, at the assembly bench end, we had a holding department where orders were set up and matched and finally packed together with stands, pedals, hihats, and whatever accessories were required. Here also was one of our main bottlenecks to the whole operation! The packed merchandise was on the third floor and the trucks outside in the alley on the ground floor. We had only a four foot by six foot elevator to convey everything down to the waiting trucks. And this elevator was wide open with just wood gates and a pull-rope for operation!

Looking back, I can see how comical this setup was. When a truck backed into the narrow 16-foot wide alley, it would sound its horn. Then the shipping clerk who was also our lone packer, would drop whatever he was working on and throw open a window in the men's washroom, and yell down at the driver. Then the elevator would be sent down to the driver and he would rise up to the third floor to make out the documents. Then both driver and shipping clerk would load up that elevator and ride down together, sometimes on top of the cartons, to the ground floor to load the truck. And no one was ever hurt and, of course, no one notified the insurance company either that this was going on.

The War In Europe Was On- Everybody Write A Book!

Since the war in Europe intensified and our government issued increasingly more restrictions, it was obvious that sooner or later our production would suffer. We met constantly trying to come up with an answer. One was that we all write a book on our specialty. Thus my father wrote *The Complete Wm. F. Ludwig Drum Instructor;* I wrote *Modern Jazz Drumming*, and together we assembled the *Wm. F. Ludwig Solo Collection.* Our sales manager Fred W. Miller even helped writing *Baton Twirling* with the help of his twirling friends. The reasoning behind all this frenetic activity was simply to survive. The books sold well, but what none of us realized at the time, was that printers seldom run their presses for anything less than 5,000 copies. So, we burdened ourselves with 15,000 instruction books which had to be paid for on delivery and severely cut into our working cash at the worst possible time.

I traveled West on a three month trip visiting every important dealer west of the Mississippi River. To save money, I teamed up with the J.C. Deagan western territory sales manager F.K. Peppler ("Pep" to the trade). We both attended the grand opening of the new Coast Wholesale Music Co.'s office and warehouse in Los Angeles. Coast also had a sister company of the same name in San Francisco.The Rocky Mountains have always been a barrier to Midwest and East Coast shippers because of the long haul out there, so it became the custom to appoint wholesalers (jobbers) exclusive for large chunks of territory in return for receiving bulk orders and warehousing space. Pep and I stored cars at alternate sites and together we drove from Los Angeles to Seattle, down to Salt Lake City (where I saw my first flights of the B-17 Flying Fortresses) back up through Idaho and we split at DesMoines. One dealer-wholesaler, Southern Music Company of San Antonio, gave me an order for six pairs of timpani in one order! Milt Fink, the owner, could see shortages coming and hedged by placing large orders in 1941 and the spring of 1942.

Winds of War

As the world became engulfed in World War II, it became evident to all of us at W.F.L. Drum Company that there were big changes coming our way. I rather frantically finished my last road trip rounding dealer calls made in my four years at approximately three hundred dealers which gave me a nice base to work from. These accounts were all plated to fit our antiquated addressograph. The mailing list also included a couple thousand dealers who were not yet buying from us as well as two thousand N.A.R.D. members we considered "prospects"– those who might buy something from us or from our dealers. (We did not sell dircct to the retail trade.)

As all-out war approached I also began a steady reduction in print advertising as well as magazine advertising.

I made one last stab at winning Gene Krupa over with a trip to New York. I met him backstage at movie houses in Camden, N.J. and Philadelphia, Pa. and became good friends with him and his gracious wife, Ethel. The Krupa band was really roaring– five shows per day starting at 11:00 A.M. and running all day. The Slingerland drums in the band were all pervasive and dealers were still answering the huge demand for Krupa drums and sticks made,of course, by Slingerland. I was wasting my time and I knew it. Finally around the end of November, I returned home and we sat around the Thanksgiving table groaning with delicious turkey and gravy prepared lovingly by my devoted mother.

It was at this time that the warships of the Imperial Japanese Fleet put to sea heading for Pearl Harbor Hawaii.

Two New Competitors Popped Up

After the attack on Pearl Harbor, The United States declared war on both Japan and Germany which increased my competition by two after Slingerland, Leedy, Ludwig & Ludwig, and Gretsch. Good grief! How much can a struggling new little drum company like W.F.L. take?

Christmas was still of good cheer with bonus checks for everyone. The babushka-covered people still changed street cars in the snow outside the plant on Damen Avenue. But there was a new feeling of tension in the air. After all, my father was born in Germany and here I was with a Germanic heritage in the largest Polish settlement outside of Warsaw! Messages were passed to us to go back to Germany. A few windows were broken. Morale began to sag.

I still made the rounds downtown. At the Blackhawk restaurant the Kay Kyser Band appeared featuring my cousin, Herman Gunkler, as first saxophone and lead clarinet player in the reed section. Eddie Shae was their drummer but completely tied into Ludwig & Ludwig.

Roy Knapp was the leading radio percussionist at the time. Roy also maintained a studio, the finest in the city at the time. Roy told me that Bud Slingerland had applied for drum lessons but that after three lessons, he gave up on him. Apparently Bud had felt our clinic programs cutting into their sales!

Meanwhile, our instruction books were beginning to come into print. I laced my book, *Modern Swing Drumming,* with lots of pictures which the Krupa book did

not have. One night, I had photographer Seymour Rudolph come to our home in River Forest and shoot all the pictures for that night, complete with my tuxedo. He then called me the next day to tell me that he had forgotten to load his camera with film! We had to do it all over again the next night which was alright as long as the drinks held out.

Business was terrific. All the groundwork, all the clinics, were finally paying off. The new catalog was pulling very well.

But now the emphasis switched, because of the war, to finding and buying raw materials.

Uncle Sam Wanted Me!

I received my draft notice on May 10th, 1942. This was indeed a surprise, since I was twenty-six years of age. I reported to the draft board in Forest Park and was sent to take my physical prior to induction in Humbolt Park. At the end of this ordeal which took all day, I was given a notice stating that I had ten days to wind up my affairs and then would be called up.

Military Service

My sister Bettie came to work at the office, as it appeared I would be gone for a while. She felt dad was alone and she volunteered to come to work for the company as his secretary. Up until that point, I had been a secretary with a pigeon-English shorthand and I wrote all of the letters. Then Bettie came in and took over that end of things.

I went up to the Great Lakes Naval base in Waukegan to see Eddie Peabody, who was a former banjo star of Ludwig &Ludwig. He was called the Banjo King. He was a lieutenant who had Sousa's old job, from WWI. I went in to see him about work. I already had a draft notice and I passed my physical for the army and I'd been told to report; I had 10 days to report to Humbolt Park fieldhouse. I walked in just as Peabody was hanging up the telephone on the admiral, having gotten chewed out for the poor deportment of the recruits on the base walking around out of step. The Admiral wanted everyone in lockstep. He told Peabody that every group over fifty should have a drummer. Peabody said, "Then you walked in..." In fact the yeoman introduced me, "Mr. Ludwig is here to see you," and he shouted, "Ludwig! send him right in!" He told me the story and I sat down. He said, "Can you teach drums?" I said, "Sure." "Can you organize drum and bugle corps?" "Yes, absolutely." "Oh, we've got to have you. Give me that notice from the army." He tore it up! He called the yeoman in and said, "We've got to get Ludwig here a rating." He looked at me and asked, " Would you take first class?" I said,

The author in his first class gob uniform. The rating is boatswains mate temporarily until the new "T" rating badges were issued. The drum is the new 12x15 single-tensioned tuneable 10% metal "Victorious" model which helped carry us through the war.

"First class sounds better than second!" So he and the yeoman went through the rating book and all they could find was buglemaster, and I couldn't play the bugle. So the yeoman said, "Sir, here's a new rating, called T for teacher." Peabody said, "That's exactly what he's going to be, teacher! We'll put him in for First class T." He gave me a note and told me to go home and I'd hear from him. In two or three days, I got a notice from the Navy Department to report to the post office. I went right up to the Great Lakes Base where I began to teach drummers.

I drove around and I organized drum and bugle corps. There were one thousand recruits arriving daily and I had my recruiters go through to check out every company for drummers and buglers. They reported to a rigging loft. There were twelve regiments, so I had twelve organizations set up. It was beautiful. They, in turn, would have these buglers and drummers lounging around waiting for assignments. Messages would come in; we have to go to the rigging loft, we have to go to swimming, we have to go to the rifle range; send over two drummers and a bugler or just two drummers. *Lockstep!!* Peabody never forgot it; he thanked me profusely, telling me I really got him out of that one. In eight weeks, I had that place marching, and they still are.

A company in that day was 120, two platoons. When you have 120 men three abreast, it stretches out quite a way and your voice won't carry that far, but a drum– that's always what a drum was for. It saved my life; I'm convinced of it.

October, 1942 regimental drum and bugle corps competition at Great Lakes Naval Training Station. The corps numbered two dozen and each performed a different routine designed and set up by the author (circled above).

A year and a half after I started, everything was going along great. I even got a call from a Lt. Commander Turick over in recruit training. He said, "My boy, I'm sorry, but your rating has been abolished. But– a new rating has been established– A for Athletics." An aircraft carrier had been sunk in the South Pacific and more men drowned from improper use of their life-saving flotation gear than from drowning. They jumped improperly from a 50-foot deck into the sea and were killed. The Navy wanted to teach everybody how to jump with their legs together and their arms crossed, like a spear. Then, once in the water, they had to know how to swim! Hardly any of the new recruits, it seemed, could swim. They built twelve olympic-size enclosed pools in one month and from then on no one could graduate unless they learned to swim and to jump from the high board with their gear on and brush simulated oil away. Many of these recruits were from Iowa; they'd never seen water! I've seen them go down and stand on the shoreline of Lake Michigan and say, "GOLLY! You can't even see the other side!!" Real Americana– farm boys, men... wonderful people but they couldn't swim a lick. They had to be hardened with exercise, so I was sent to another camp in Maryland called Bainbridge and taught to be a Chief Petty Officer, one rank upwards, and direct calisthenics. After two months, we graduated com-

Packing field drums made for the government. Four thousand were made in 1943 and 1944. These instruments were exempt from the War Production Board's "10%" decree.

pletely reuniformed. I was sent back to Great Lakes because commander Turick sent for me. I was one of two called back while the others were sent to the Aleutians or the Solomon Islands; terrible places. I spent the duration pushing companies as a commander complete with calisthenics and rifle drills. I always had the best companies because of drumming. One hundred and twenty men completely in unison! My companies were always requested on mainside for reviews to accompany visitors because they were sharp, and that comes from rhythm. Many times I had to march my company to fire drills where they had a flaming building. Men had to march for miles to Waukegan, then go in and spray, etc. Often I'd ask a soldier for his drum and I'd play *The Downfall of Paris*, or *The Connecticut Halftime* and they loved it. I was there until 1945. The recruits said they could always tell when I took over the field drum. Such is the power of the rudiments!

On one of my wartime visits to W.F.L., I observed the wood shop bending wood chair backs at one cent each in our bending machines. The order was for 100,000 chair backs to be bent to fit the contour of the human body. It wasn't drum building, but it kept some money coming in and alive for the future. No one EVER thought we would lose that war! Except in the beginning when Imperial Japan was running wild in the Pacific arena.

The 1943 promotion to Chief Petty Officer

W.F.L. endorser Buddy Schutz with a war-time drum set sans bass drum, on horseback. This photo was taken during the filming of an Abbott & Costello feature film for which Jimmy Dorsey's band got the contract. The script called for the sheik's orchestra and retinue to march into Baghdad.

Wm. F. Ludwig Sr. poses with the "drums" made for the show *Ice Capades of 1942*. The show featured one hundred skaters–mostly women. They ordered, and W.F.L. delivered, making up 100 none-tunable very light weight drums without snares. The shells were two-ply; one ply poplar and one panel of maple. The fake wood lugs were screwed to the hoops and heavy cardboard was affixed in place of heads. Colored cord adorned each drum. The "drums" were not to be played.

WFL's first attempt at building a complete five-piece set using only 10% metal or less.

The shells for the "Victorious" kit were constructed in our usual three-ply cross-grained construction. Two panels of long-grain African mahogany were laid up with a thick panel of cross grain poplar in the center. This provided WFL's typical light weight but exceedingly strong construction. Each shell was reinforced with solid maple glue rings.

The solid maple hoops were tensioned using stamped double claw hooks inserted into steel threaded nuts embedded in the hollowed-out wooden lugs. These lugs were hand cut on a band saw using rock maple and then stained brown to offset the marine pearl plastic finish. The lower head on each of the three tom toms was enclosed with a goatskin head, tacked with a double row of tacks. The wooden hi hat pedal depended on a cord to close the upper cymbal against the lower cymbal. The snare drum is made entirely of maple, as is the pedal and tom tom legs. The tom tom holders were constructed from very thin steel. The cow bell was of steel, of course, but the tone block on the left was injection molded plastic with two steel tuning pegs. Several hundred of these sets were sold before being discontinued in 1943 as unstable. A new Ray Bauduc instruction book was included with each set as shown.

Mr. H.N. White died at the beginning of the war, leaving his widow to struggle with keeping the huge business operating in very difficult times. My father volunteered to act as a temporary executive vice-president. He and my mother packed up and moved to Cleveland in 1944, leaving Fred Miller in charge of the drum plant with its dozen or so employees. (Mr. Strupe joined my father in the move to Cleveland, making any engineering at the drum factory during the war years very difficult.) The White Company managed to survive the war contracting war work as a subcontractor to the larger firms. Much of WFL's work was also subcontracting; I recall an order for 10,000 machine gun locks. Somehow the "guys" survived those four terrible years!

Back To Work– Post War Rebuilding

The year 1946 dawned on a world at peace. Europe and most of Japan lay in ruins. And W.F.L. Drum Company was not much better.

My father returned from his temporary position with the H.N.White Company and I returned from Great Lakes Naval Training station older, but not neccessarily wiser.

I began again as I had nine years before with a catalog. This one featured a parade and encouraged veterans to join up and fly our country's flag "down America's broad avenues". This was stupid on the face of it. Veterans returning from long absences from families and friends were not about to spend any time march-ing. But it went to print that way and everything sold out in a month due to material shortages. Plus we had to rebuild our work force which numbered a couple of dozen at this point in 1946 and we had nearly 100 people before the war. Hiring qualified workers was highly competitive in the shop as well as the office.

I saw an ad for a new electric IBM typewriter and answered it resulting in a sales call and a brand new machine which was delightful to operate. My father caught sight of it and without asking the price said, "Send it back." I cajoled, I pleaded, I pointed out the many advantages of the electric system over pushing manual keys. He was unmoved so I had to call the salesman back to pick up the machine. As that salesman grappled with reinserting the machine back in the shipping box, my father swiveled, rocked, and puffed his cigar in pleasure. With sweat pouring off that salesman's brow he looked up at my father and said, "Mr. Ludwig, it's people like you that cause recessions!" I never forgot that statement. But Dad had saved $500.00 to put into something else for the shop that he figured was more important.

The New Die-Cast Lugs

One of the very first engineering jobs to be tackled was a new line of tension casings. Our Strupe line of stamped tension casings were ugly and ragged due to heavy wear during the war years. So a new line of die cast lugs was designed distinct and apart from anything the competition fielded. Casting about for a name, I thought "classic" would reflect the new look. That design served us well for more than fifty years! And of course a new strainer, the "classic" strainer, had to be developed. Most of all, we needed a replacement engineer for Mr. Strupe who passed away in Cleveland that year. This is a key position if not THE key position in any organization– chief engineer. It is also the highest paying and most difficult to fill. It isn't that there are shortages of engineers– it's that there is always a shortage of GOOD

Spring, 1946, renewed a flood of prominent visitors to our factory. Here the percussion section of the Boston Symphony Orchestra inspects the first post-war timpani production. The last army order is stacked up in the background!

engineers! And we hired and fired, hired and fired for many years. The ones we didn't fire, quit. This went on for years. Oh, for another Strupe, or, heaven grant us another R.C. Danly! But it never happened. Some were overqualified.Many underqualified but good at writing a resume and selling themselves. But all contributed something and when closely supervised, did produce some ideas and improved machinery. Engineering falls into more than one category– there are design engineers, machinery engineers, production engineers and usually each person specializes in only one field. It is nearly impossible to get one that combines all three fields. So we had to make the best of it. One after another, they paraded through the plant, some contributing a little something, others nothing, and, worst of all, some taking us in the wrong direction. It was indeed frustrating and probably still is.

Finally the new Classic line was delivered and I proceeded to line up the drummer with Ray Anthony's swing band with the first of the new Classic marine pearl outfits. This was a co-op deal with the H.N. White Co., as Ray used the King trumpet– White's first line horn.We got some business from this.

The Origin Of The Midwest Band Clinic

One day in August of 1946, I picked up the phone in our small office and it was Howard Lyons. He was the CEO and President of the Lyons Band Instrument Company located at 333 West Lake Street in the loop of Chicago. He outlined the purpose of his call which was to get from me a pair of our pedal tuned timpani, a concert bass drum with stand, and the necessary beaters to go with them. The Lyons Company had invited about thirty five band directors from around Chicago to come to the store the week before Christmas to play through some new music. Howard said the invitees would bring their own instruments and Lyons would supply whatever was missing from stock.

I immediately agreed to provide those percussion instruments first because Lyons was a really big customer and, second, because Christmas was a long way off from August. How many times have you agreed to some event far in the distance?

The Lyons Company under the very visionary leadership of the brothers, Howard and William, who did the books, ran a mail order business nationally and were one of the first organizations to promote band and orchestra formation through easy payment plans. In addition, they held meetings in schools (with parents present) extolling the advantages of school music activities. Most schools throughout our nation already had choral programs but precious few in the country had money for expensive musical instruments. Band instrument recruitment was developed into a real science. Lyons had three full time recruitment men on the road most of the time. On an appointed evening, parents and children would arrive at the school auditorium or gym and the Lyons band rep would sell them on joining a band. The Lyons man picked up each individual instrument, described it, and often played it, even if only for a few notes. Then the audience was asked to stand and form lines at tables with the instruments of their choice. Brass instrument applicants had to have straight teeth while those with an overbite were fitted for a reed instrument like a clarinet or oboe. Next came the pricing of the instruments and the time payment purchasing plan, usually ten dollars down and ten per month. Then the Lyons Company would supply a list of available band and orchestra directors who the school board could approach on their own. In other words, the Lyons brothers were *band builders*, not just salesmen.

With this system, the company carried no less than 35,000 accounts on their books and all this when a computer was a sharp pencil or pen!

A request from Howard or Bill, therefore, was practically an order! I felt honored to receive the request before Slingerland; it was another large step toward fulfillment of The Plan! (Concentrate on school business.) When the time came, I loaded the timps and concert size bass drum in the company's wood-body station wagon and set course, through the deep snow of the latest blizzard, for Lake Street. Upon arrival, I found the way blocked front and back of the Lyons store by giant snowdrifts, some four to five feet high. With help from some of the store personnel, we cut a path through the snow and practically dragged them through the doors. I attended this First Midwest Clinic because there was a shortage of a bass drummer and also to meet the directors. Howard let me put up a W.F.L. banner. The directors played through a raft of new band music, some published by Ludwig Music Publishing Company of Cleveland, Ohio (no relation) and other publishers. It was a huge success. And all left with a request that there be a second clinic the next year.

In January, Howard called up again with a request to come down and pick up the timpani and bass drum. I told him he should keep them in stock. His response was, "We can't. We're taking inventory and we want them out of here!" I was crushed but couldn't argue with the customer, so again went down in the wagon, plodded through the snowdrifts, dragged the beasts out, loaded up, and went back to the factory on Damen Avenue. But I got a nice letter from the Lyons Brothers with the invitation to supply the percussion instruments next year, 1947. For the next fifty years, we were privileged to supply all of the percussion instruments for the Midwest Band and Orchestra clinics, a tradition that continues to this day. Fully $100,000 wholesale of twelve timps, three concert bass drums, many marimbas and vibes, and also accessories– stands, holders, you name it! Through over fifty years since the first Midwest Clinic in the old Lyons Band Instrument store with just 35 band directors,the clinic had grown to gigantic proportions. I have given many clinics also as well as supplied all the percussion instruments. The dozens of bands and orchestras traveling to the Hilton Hotel on Michigan Avenue never had to bring their own timpani or drums. I saw that they were on stage and tuned up ready to play.

The Hilton Hotel is one of the largest in the country, with nearly 3,000 rooms. Since the event is always held the week before Christmas as Howard Lyons decreed it would be, the entire hotel is gaily festooned from top to bottom with glorious Christmas decorations. But, as usual, I'm getting ahead of myself. Back to the the third clinic in 1949 which was held in a hotel, the Sherman House, for the first time. Howard Lyons allowed the music publishers to exhibit for the first time. In the following three years, only publishers of what the trade refers to as software were allowed to exhibit. (Software refers to printed music and accessories, as opposed to hardware which refers to actual instruments.) In the fourth year, I applied to exhibit and was accepted, as we published instruction books. Naturally, I supplied a practice pad and sticks in order to demonstrate the drum figures and solos in the books. Slingerland complained bitterly and it was on this complaint that Howard Lyons opened up the entire display space to instrument and other hardware manufacturers.

One year, 1959, I believe, my arch-rival, Bud Slingerland, demanded that Howard Lyons give him the opportunity to supply all the percussion instruments and since the Lyons Company also sold Slingerland, Howard was hard-pressed to turn Bud Slingerland down. So Howard agreed and I was informed that Slingerland would supply *all* the percussion instruments that year and that the J.C. Deagan Company would supply all the marimbas, xylophones, bells, and chimes. We still had our big W.F.L. display in place as usual. I got a call from one of the main conductors in the middle of the Midwest Clinic week pleading, "Bill, for God's sake rush down some timpani and real drums we can perform on. All Bud Slingerland sent was Boy Scout stuff!" I said, "No problem." I then proceeded to turn the plant upside down and we worked some departments overtime to assemble timpani and concert drums to rush down the next morning.

At 6:00 A.M., the wonderful Jim Griggs, owner of the Griggs trucking service which all music houses in the city used to transport musical instruments, met me at our shipping room door. We loaded up, and at 8:00 A.M., our truck was at the Hilton Hotel door (then named the Stevens Hotel, I believe) and I had the distinct pleasure, and I mean *pleasure*, of removing every bit of Slingerland equipment from all stages in use including rehearsal hall and replacing it with our brand new shining professional timpani and drums. It was a major triumph. I made certain that the word spread throughout that year's Midwest Clinic! William Revelli, the director of the Midwest Clinic and also director of bands and orchestras at the University of Michigan, hugged me.

I was told a very beaten and chastised Bud Slingerland came to the hotel to find out what happened. Everybody razzed him. I was in heaven!

Now there are times when you are beaten down so far you can't even see daylight. And then there are times you are soaring on the winds of victory. That's life, of course– down, then up. But nothing before or since even came close to resembling that victory at the 1959 Midwest Band and Orchestra Clinic!

Today there are some seven hundred companies displaying their wares at the Midwest Clinic in the Hilton Hotel in Chicago. There are dozens of bands and orchestras traveling from all over our nation and some as far away as Japan to perform new music for thousands of educators. And we still supply all the percussion instruments! It's a record I am proud of and a long haul from the snowdrifts of that first clinic long ago– the brainchild of a genius named Howard Lyons!

The Plan Realized
It was now over a half century since the first concept of The Plan appeared in my mind as I drove West in the setting afternoon sun returning from my first road trip East. I felt The Plan was indeed fulfilled for it was said you could walk into any high school or college in the land and find Ludwig timpani or drums on stage. It was something you could bet on!

Conventions Return
The first of the postwar trade shows was held in Cleveland, Ohio, so we featured the Classic line at our display. But what I recall most about this 1946 show was another example of the futility of over-demonstrating a product. The reader will recall my struggle with reassembling a timpani at the Enid, Oklahoma, band festival. Being attracted to the Grossman Music Co. exhibit by the crowd, I squeezed in to see that was going on. I found the owner, Henry Grossman himself, demonstrat-

ing their new all-plastic trumpet. At the end of his demo he smashed it on the end of a table to stress durability and it broke into five pieces! Everyone froze and my mind went immediately back to Enid, Oklahoma. I felt sorry for Henry. He stood there for a few minutes with his broken horn in his hand then slowly the crowd dispersed without another word. Lesson repeated– never over-demonstrate your product. And that goes for playing as well. When you have your audience in the palm of your hand, that's the time to start thinking about your exit!

Post War Prosperity

The pent-up demand for products following the war

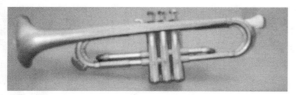

Ed. note: The plastic trumpet referred to by the author was designed by the brilliant (yet fallible) Joe Thompson, the man responsible for the tremendously successful Rogers drum innovations of the 1960s.

Sometimes competitors met in a hospitable atmosphere at music conventions. Front row: Fred Miller of WFL, Maurie Lishon of Franks Drum Shop. Back row: George Way of George Way Drums, the author, Joe Berryman of Ludwig & Ludwig, Larry Rohlfing of Leedy.

was enormous. We were inundated with orders. Hardly a day passed without a personal visit from some dealer or jobber placing huge orders, mostly for outfits. Since the company had been making four-piece mahogany sets for the services under Government contracts, we continued to make four-piece outfits, but in lacquer colors. In fact, we developed a hair-brained attitude that we would just make drum sets on into eternity.

A drum set consists of stands, a pedal, spurs, tom tom holder and legs, sticks, and an instruction book (mine). That meant manufacturing a lot of metal parts, since we were set up from the beginning to make everything ourselves "within the confines of these four walls," as my father constantly drummed into us. (No pun intended.) We ran the company flat out at full speed five and a half days per week, swallowing the overtime expense a half day on Saturday.

I remember standing alone at dusk on the shipping floor during my lockup rounds and observing a couple of field drums slated for Coast Wholesale Music Company of San Francisco. They were finished in beautiful gold lacquer that shimmered in the setting sun pouring through the dusty factory windows. What attracted my attention especially to these two drums was the wavy edges of the steel lugs holding the tension rods. They were just awful! Obviously the dies and the punch press were severely worn. I was glad these two drums were going far away– the West Coast! This thought was immediately followed by another dreadful one. How long will our customers stand for such lousy quality? The image of those two golden drums haunted me for the rest of my life as a drummaker and I resolved this must not happen again any more than frozen hams bouncing off office desks in 1941! I pushed ever harder on replacing those stamped lugs with the new die cast lug line. These finally began arriving in 1947.

Another problem was lack of adequate space, so I engineered the purchase of the house next door and we altered it to our needs including our first warehouse for receiving raw materials on the ground floor of that building. But none of the floors matched our factory floors, so there was a good deal of lifting and moving involved in using the new space efficiently.

My Involvement with Buddy Rich

The war years saw many changes, one of which was the decline in interest in Dixieland music. The Crosby

44

Band had disbanded leaving me with two name drummers still on the road– Buddy Schutz with Jimmy Dorsey and Frankie Carlson with Woody Herman. Realizing the boom wouldn't last forever, I thought we had better start rebuilding our artist inventory. That was in line with the need to rebuild every department in the post world war period.

Buddy had formed his own band in Los Angeles. I heard they were training to Chicago on the luxury Santa Fe Chief train. I decided to meet that train.

Everyone in the organization tried to dissuade me– my father, our sales manager, Fred Miller, our factory manager, Fritz Kiemle. My father never spoke about the Rich affiliation of the 1920s. Fred Miller had been there in the Ludwig & Ludwig office during the late 20s and said that the Rich act had played Chicago about once a year. Whenever they did, Senior Rich would bring young Buddy out to the factory to be measured (yes, that's right, *measured*) for a new bass drum. This was their attempt to keep Buddy small behind the bass drum, as in the photo of *Traps, The Drum Wonder*. (He used to open the show playing a solo while totally concealed by the bass drum.) Buddy, according to Fred, was always snarly and was often seen kicking his old man in the shins. His constant obnoxious behavior grated on everyone's nerves. Eventually the bass drum upsizing

**Wm. F. Ludwig Sr. and Buddy Rich
toast a deal signing**

ended with a 16x36 drum which caused shipping problems for the traveling act. It is that final size that is shown in the 1929 photo of Buddy playing in the Vitaphone movie short. He had outgrown the drum at that point.

Again, I can never remember my father mentioning his association with Buddy Rich in the teens or 1920s. I suppose the endorsement just petered out with the demise of vaudeville in general.

I persisted, with the argument that if we had to begin asking for orders again we should be ready and prepare now. The Chief arrived early one morning and I was there. I looked for Bud Slingerland who had taken over Slingerland upon his father's death in 1946, but didn't see him. I found Buddy and his female companion and offered a ride to the Sherman House which he gratefully accepted. Being met by anyone upon reaching a destination pleases everyone! Upon checking into the suite, I launched my campaign to get him off Slingerland and on to W.F.L.. My main argument was that with Slingerland he would always be number two on the totem pole whereas with us, he would be number one. Secondly, we were geared up for our first big advertising promotion since the war ended and were prepared to feature him if he would only give his approval. He agreed to look at the ad materials and we made a date to meet on opening night.

Buddy Rich Opens in Chicago

The Panther Room in Chicago's Sherman House was a glittering room featuring animal motifs. Upholstery, artwork, menus, bar area, everything reminded one of panthers– those wild jungle beasts. Consequently, having Buddy open there with his new band was an extremely festive occasion. Opening night saw the place packed. The waiting line extended up the stairs into the main floor lobby above. The band was loud and great! It was so loud it was hard to carry on a conversation. I looked for Bud Slingerland. He was nowhere to be seen. What luck! Between sets I congratulated Buddy on his success and called attention to Slingerland's lack of attention in not appearing. I told Buddy I had a massive advertising campaign ready to kick off and I thought we should meet in his suite the next day. He agreed.

The Buddy Rich Campaign

For our meeting, I brought several full-page layouts featuring Buddy in a variety of poses. In addition I was able to point out that we also made a full line of timpani which would be available to him whenever he was in the Chicago area. To start with, we could send down to the Panther Room *right now* three pairs of pedal-tuned timpani for his use the entire duration of his two week engagement. Again I hammered on the theme that as long as he stayed with Slingerland he would be number two. At first he was undecided, but after a second meeting in which I brought an unwilling father along, he agreed to switch brands of drums. I drafted a letter addressed to Slingerland, notifying them of Buddy's decision. That night Bud Slingerland showed up at the Panther Room but he was too late; I had Buddy signed up.

The six timpani were delivered, making a more crowded backstage than usual.Buddy worked the timps into his act very skillfully and man, it was loud!

An Unhappy Manager

The maitre d' and manager of the room was Ernie Byfield. He was a very important part of Chicago's entertainment scene, being also the manager of the famous Ambassador East dining room. One night I went with Buddy to see Ernie at the entrance which was his customary post every evening. Ernie asked if Buddy could tone the volume down on the first set so the dinner guests could more easily converse. Buddy replied, "Here– you take the #$%&*@ sticks and go lead the band and I'll act as maitre d' and seat the people." I was stunned. The manager was making a simple request: tone the band down for the first set. Buddy's answer was to play louder than ever. In fact he even moved the timpani solo up to the first set– just the opposite of what was desired. Byfield was furious. He told me that Buddy would never play there again, and he didn't. This was my first view of Buddy Rich's personality and I began to wonder what kind of "ride" my tiger would give me!

Naturally I featured Buddy on the cover of the next two catalogs; one with a red cover and the other green. I also increased the size of both, which provided better layout possibilities. We catalogued Buddy Rich snare drums, outfits, and sticks. This way we were able to track the value of our investment which was considerable. Both catalogs were accepted enthusiastically by the trade. The year 1949 closed at $725,000.00 in sales with a net profit of $21,300.00, or 2.9%. The addition of Buddy Rich to our endorsee list would cost the company 34 drums the first year. He was very hard on his drums, but not that hard! What happened? He gave them away. If he took a fancy to some bartender in one of the joints,he thought nothing of leaving his set when the job was finished. This included cases as well. He then would call or have his roadie call for more drums. If I objected and asked what happened to the set he left behind, he would often get on the phone himself and burn up the wires for questioning his need for another set, ending with, "You got that, bird-brain?" That was the second

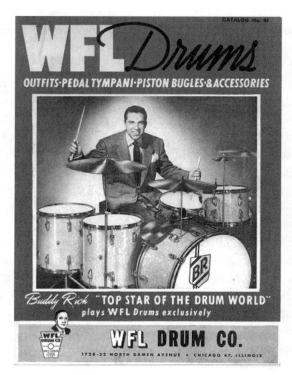

WFL Catalog #49, 1949

time in my life I had been referred to as a bird's brain and I was beginning to wonder if it was true! Buddy's set was not exactly standard. The drums were right off the assembly line, but the drilling for holders was very special, as was the head selection and front bass drum painting. Since he would be without a set and on the road, haste was an absolute neccessity.

To solve this ongoing problem, we learned to make up and hold in stock three complete marine pearl Buddy Rich sets in cases. I never mustered up the courage to complain and the free giveaways continued. I have to laugh today when I read about someone who has one of these sets and is trying to attach a special monetary value to it when there has to be several dozen out there. I know; I wrote the orders up– all of them!

We designed a special Buddy Rich stick for him. It was a takeoff on our model 1A. We were a long time getting it to his liking– about a year. Having Buddy Rich imprinted on the shank meant a lot to the thousands of Buddy Rich fans.

Rich was brilliant and now that he was fronting his own big band, he was the ideal counterweight to Slingerland's long ride with Gene Krupa and his band. There were actually two camps of young people; those who thought one was better than the other– Rich or Krupa.

Riding The Rich Tiger

The next ten years or so having Buddy as our lead

endorser may have been profitable but it sure wore me out! Whenever he appeared in the Chicago area, I always made it a point to be there on opening night whether with a band or quartet or with somebody else's group like Norman Granz's "Jazz at The Philharmonic" (JATP).

Slowly, almost inperceptively, the public taste for big band music was shifting to a taste for small groups. This, together with the lack of cooperation from Rich in considering the wishes of the clubs or ballrooms caused job offers to decline at an alarming rate. One incident stands out in my mind. Buddy and his big band were appearing for one night at a ballroom in Gary, Indiana–practically a suburb of Chicago. I was there, of course. Unfortunately there were very few patrons and they had obviously come to dance and watch the soloists. During an intermission, the manager of this ballroom came to Buddy with what I thought was a simple request. He asked if the band could play a few slow dreamy tunes for the young dancers who wanted to dance. You guessed it. Buddy whipped out his sticks, offering them to the manager with the words, "Here, Mister. You play the drums and lead my band and I'll collect the tickets!" After a few seconds of an embarassing standoff, Buddy returned to the band and proceeded to play for the rest of the evening the loudest and fastest numbers in the book. That manager told me, "Never again!" and I thought to myself, "He's killing his own market!" At the end of that engagement, Buddy called the band together and gave each of them five dollars with instructions to get to the next gig (in Milwaukee) on their own.

The One And Only Buddy Rich W.F.L. Clinic Tour

It wasn't long before dates dried up altogether and when next I saw Buddy, he was setting up his outfit on stage at the Chicago Opera House for a performance with JATP. Entrepreneur Norman Granz appeared and immediately lashed out at me for not taking advantage of Buddy's appearances with the group. His position was that I should set up clinics in every city where they would appear. I told him I would be glad to, with Buddy's agreement. I turned to Buddy who was still struggling with spur placement on his set and asked, "Is this what you want to do?" Buddy answered with a very subdued, "I guess so." I turned back to Granz and asked, "What if he doesn't show up?" His reply, "I'll give you $50.00 for every clinic date Buddy misses." I thought that was a good deal for me and the company. The next day I went back to my office and proceeded to book ten clinic dates, one for each of the towns they would appear in. It was a catastrophe. Half of the dates he kept, I wished he had not appeared. In the first clinic, which was in India-

napolis, he punched out the leading drummer in town at the clinic after an argument on closing the roll. At the next, in Houston, he played one riff and advised the audience to come to the concert to hear the rest. This after Herb Brochstein, the drum department manager of H & H Music Company, had spent the better part of the day setting up an exact duplicate of Buddy's outfit and rented four hundred chairs! (Herbie Brochstein later founded Pro Mark stick company.) If Buddy felt good enough to play, as he did at the Dallas clinic, he brought the house down. At others, such as Fort Worth, he did not always provide the best product endorsements. The Speed King pedal link broke during the clinic in Fort Worth. He picked up the pedal and hurled it off the stage.

Catastrophe In San Antonio, Texas

I was cleaning up my day's work at the office when the phone rang. It was Milt Fink of Southern Music Company asking, "Where's your boy?" I was dumbfounded but knew right away that Buddy was a no-show again, at the biggest turnout of the tour. Milt had gone all out and had five hundred people in a nearby auditorium he had rented for the occasion. The clinic was set to start at 3:00 P.M.. When Buddy failed to show up, Milt's drum man, Fred Hoey, stepped in and gave a two-hour clinic. There were people in that audience who had left home at dawn to drive across that part of Texas . That night Milt and Fred Hoey went backstage and accosted Rich. His excuse was that the plane from New York City was delayed and what was he supposed to do, jump out at 10,000 feet? From that day on, Southern Music Company tore the front page off our catalogs for the rest of the time we featured Buddy on the cover. That tragic incident taught me yet another bitter lesson– never put any artist on the front cover, even if he is the greatest in the world. It also taught me to suspend arranging clinics with Buddy Rich. He was utterly unreliable. Norman Granz owes me $250.00!

The Buddy Rich Secret

Buddy was not always garrulous. He had his lighter moments, although there seemed to be very few around me. In one of those moments, he leaned over and asked with a twinkle in his eyes, "Want to be in on a secret?" "Yes," I replied. "Watch my feet! You only watch my hands like everybody else–my chops. I'm not playing the drums– I'm dancing on them!" Then he reminded me of his baby years where his first lessons were not on the drums. They were tap dancing lessons! When he was two years of age he was watching his parents' song and dance vaudeville act and learning the steps. As soon as he could, they included him in their act. So I did as he

47

said, and sure enough, in his solo, his feet would rise up on both bass drum and hi hat pedal and he would swing into a toe to heel to toe tap dance rhythm and the beater would bounce off the bass head in those flam accents he was famous for. I guess we should all take tap lessons along with our drum lessons! Buddy was proud of the fact that he never took a drum lesson in his life and was fond of so stating to any and all teachers in the audience in clinic situations. This did nothing but infuriate all teachers of drumming in his audiences.

On the plus side of Buddy Rich playing WFL drums, he was really one of a kind. I always liked the crisp tension on his #400 snare drum. And the way he tuned his set in pleasing intervals of thirds.... all four drums. And his execution was always crystal clear. In twenty years or so of watching and listening to him, I never detected an error. In playing "fours" he would get himself so involved that it seemed utterly impossible he would come out in time. But every time in the last millisecond he would arrive in time with a heavy cymbal crash. It was like magic to me. There never was any hesitation; it was always go– go– go, and drive, drive! He set the standard by which all percussionists were to be measured for all eternity.

A Touch of Rich Humility

Once playing with JATP, a battle of drums was scheduled featuring Gene Krupa against Buddy Rich. It was a little unfair because it was set at a time when Gene was well past his prime and Buddy was definitely at his peak of power. Naturally Buddy "carved" Gene and very badly. Everyone was embarrassed. Finally, in between fours, Gene pretended to drop a stick and in the silence that followed, whispered, "Mercy." It was fairly audible in the front rows where I was sitting. Buddy very gallantly acknowledged this plea and for rest of that "battle" played down to Gene's level! I still think that this was the most magnificent and gracious act I've ever seen in all of drumming.

Those prominent show people are different than you and I. You can't blame them, I guess. In my classical piano years, I always heard that the great German composer Ludwig Van Beethoven was extremely temperamental. That's part of being a genius! Buddy did have his touches of humility, and when he did he was absolutely charming and engaging.

The Rich association of the 1940s and 1950s cost the company about 30 to 40 drums per year but no cash ever changed hands. That came later when Henry Grossman of the Grossman Music Company (large wholesalers in Cleveland, Ohio) paid Rich $10,000 cash to play Rogers. That was the start in the percussion field of "payola". For that kind of money you could buy anybody.

400 Timps, Anybody? What Am I Offered?

In 1947 the United States Quartermaster Department in Philadelphia, Pennsylvania, issued an invitation to bid on 200 pairs of timpany, pedal tuned, with trunks. Naturally, it took my breath away to say the least. In my imagination I could visualize 400 timpani in a row even when driving my car. Nothing like this had ever occured in the history of music. The only timpani specifications the Army had were for a pair of timpani *horse mounted*. Two hundred pedal-tuned pairs almost defied the imagination!

I took the bid home on a weekend and wore out a couple pencils figuring costs to arrive at the lowest possible price to get that bid. I virtually threw the trunks in for free, just charging my costs. Then I looked up Leedy & Ludwig's prices– the only other timpani manufacturers around. I completed all the forms, submitted my bid, and waited. The person in charge of the quartermaster department was Earl Cochran and he was to call me when the decision was reached. He did. I lost. Slingerland Drum Company got the bid, even though they had never built a timp in their lives! That was the new president of Slingerland Drum Company; Bud Slingerland replacing his deceased father, H.H. Slingerland. I couldn't believe it. I hurt in my heart and it was many years before I started to get over it. This episode was my first loss to Bud Slingerland and so we became glorious enemies!

1947– The author and father with a stack of post-war bass drums.

48

These are some of the pains one must handle in business. Our only consolation was that the timpani were poorly designed and poorly received by the army. I ran into some of them at Army posts in my travels. One set was up at Fort Sheridan, forty miles north of Chicago. They called me for help when one of their timpani heads broke. I found when I arrived that the flesh hoops were aluminum and the distorted tension of the head on the calf skin heads pulling against the weak aluminum open-ended flesh hoops caused the rip. I sold them a replacement head mounted on a W.F.L. cadmium steel welded hoop.

Either Read The Bids Or Quit Bidding

My next bid on a government contract occured in early 1950. The Army wanted 100 slings, O.D. (Olive Drab) and I had bid these before. Again I would be bidding against Bud Slingerland, Gretsch, Leedy, and Ludwig & Ludwig. I bid my regular low sling price and was astonished to receive a telegram back from the quartermaster department: "Your bid lowest for 100 slings." "A little extra business never hurt anyone," I thought, "and besides, I know their credit is good." I fished the bid out of my "pending" files, read it, and dumped it into the work order file. In doing so, I turned it face down and noticed, to my horror, detailed drawings I had not seen before. In studying it further, I found that what they wanted was flag pole slings, each with a leather strap and very expensive brass holding cup for the flag staff. I immediately called my friend Earl Cochran at quartermaster heaquarters and explained my dilemma. He said I would have to appear before the whole purchasing board in person, which I did. This board sat at the longest, largest table I had ever seen in my life. At the end was a three-star general. I stood at the other end at attention totally petrified and sweating it out. I explained the difference between a drum sling for $.90 and the estimated cost of a flag-carrying sling which was about $9.90. We would lose nearly $9,000.00 if we had to buy them from the previous supplier to fulfill my contractual error. After some minutes during which the purchasing officers conferred, the general spoke up: "Young man, if you intend to bid on Government contracts in the future, you had better read them in detail." Case dismissed. I stuttered a grateful, "Thank you, sir." and got quickly out of there, I tell you!

We finished the year 1951 with $835,600 in sales and a profit of $26,700; approximately 3%. We were making progress slowly but surely. The trouble was we were plowing it all back into the business, leaving not much for bonuses (none) and salaries (little). But that is true of all growing businesses. Now, though, I could command a raise to $135 per week! I was now living alone, having finally been able to afford to move out of my parents' River Forest house to a small house in nearby Elmwood Park. I devoted my free time to night life visits to *all* the drummers in Chicago's bustling loop.

Night Life In Chicago's Loop– 1950

There were thirty or more night spots hosting live music in those days. Three of them featured "name" bands or groups. In addition the four big movie houses still featured live shows between film features. I had a warm acquaintance with all the backstage guards so I could catch the drummers as they came off the stage and these were five to six show days! I arranged for dozens of drummers in the 1950s to trade their outfits for brand new WFL sets. (Ludwig sets when we got our name back.) One of my regulars was Barrett Deems who billed himself as the world's fastest drummer. Whenever Buddy met Barrett he made him back down on that claim. Me? I stayed out of that one but inwardly I knew who was the cleanest and crispest– Buddy, of course! But I humored Barrett to keep him in line. Since all the deals, and I mean *all*, were trades, drum for drum, I ended up with a bunch of old drums in our already crowded shipping room. Being too cheap to destroy them, I pedaled them in the neighborhood– very carefully indeed! (We were forbidden to sell anything retail or could lose the dealer's loyalty.)

The Elmwood Park House; author's home 1947–-1954

Plant Expansion

As the stacks of bass drums in the photograph on page 48 indicate, business was good in the decade after the war's end. I wanted an addition to our factory. Dad didn't. He was still traumatized by his first factory expansion in the first company, Ludwig & Ludwig, and he didn't want to be caught over-extended again.

So I reverted to plotting. He liked to vacation from two to three weeks a year in Florida. The following year after they left to drive to Key Biscayne, Florida, I disconnected all power to the house next door and called in some wreckers. By the time he returned, the house was half demolished and he was furious. It isn't easy working for your father but we had to get along for the sake of the business.

We then jointly signed a contract with a local builder for the construction of a three story addition for $50,000.00. Our first loan, and a big one at that. This addition doubled our floor space and we just oozed into it floor by floor, even before the roof was finished.

The sales for the year 1953 were $880,220.00, with a net profit after taxes of $18,188.00, or 2%. Dividends

The author putting the ax to the first of 27 buildings that would eventually be wrecked to make room for factory expansions.

One of the three-flats that had to be brought down to yield access to the land for plant expansion.

Complete factory addition (circled) followed by additional wrecking to get at the land.

50

paid to the owners amounted to $7,500.00. It should be obvious to the reader that all our work, all our effort was mainly a labor of love. We still celebrated each April first as another year in business and a victory over our crosstown foe, Slingerland. There was now no question we would survive!

A Big New Catalog

The 1953 catalog featured Wm. F. Ludwig Sr. and the heading "Here's my best in 50 years." It was a blockbuster! The opening pages featured beautiful multi-color outfits followed by Buddy Rich and sets on pages 3 and 4. No more artists on the cover! I continued my loop calls and added several new "name" drummers: Roy Haynes, Stan Levy, Ray McKinley, Paul Whiteman Jr., Cozy Cole, and our first female drum star, Viola Smith, with the all girl band led by Phil Spitalny. The first line of field drums in full pearl sparkling colors concluded this forty-four page colorful book. Bugles were also included, with the new valve pistons which we bought locally from the Wm. Frank Company..

Drums Sizes Change With The Times

It all started with Buddy Rich requesting a reduction in his bass drum size from 28" down to 26". I asked him why. He said, "I think the sound is better and certainly easier to carry around." I think it was because he was now traveling with a four man group as the demand for big 18-piece bands diminished at the same time that costs skyrocketed. That meant that we had better listen up and start reducing some sizes on our catalog outfits! Another change we made when we expanded into the new building at 1730-32 North Damen Ave. was to begin mounting shell-mount holders on the outfits. (This meant shell-mount spurs, as well.)

Chaos In The Plant

The day we were to change over to shell mount everything was the day everything came to a halt. We had not prepared adequately and the departments involved were attempting to drill holes in shells using only rulers and eye sighting. Consequently few holders fit those holes! We cut up and threw out several dozen bass drum and tom tom shells before the boys got the hang of it and then proceeded to tool up with jigs and

guides for the assemblers. That was one of the worst weeks of my life and left a string of tattered nerves and ruined work in its wake. Believe it or not, it took fully a month to smooth out the glitches from changing over from hoop-mount holders to the shell-mount holders. Lesson: Whatever your estimated time is for completion of a project– double it!

Music Festival Leads to Marriage

In the spring of 1954, I received a phone call from Homer Luther, our dealer in Ponca City, Oklahoma, asking if I was coming to the Tri State Music Festival in nearby Enid. I answered that I was planning on it. Homer invited me to stop by his store and give a clinic

Mrs. Wm. F. Ludwig II (Maggie) beams happily after being awarded the LUDWIG MERIT AWARD MEDAL, a special award presented to deserving drummers for many years.She was most instrumental in influencing important dealers and acted as hostess at all convention receptions.

51

for the "Big Blue" High School Band and percussion section and said he wanted me to meet one of his employees. I readily accepted, and arrived May 5th at his door in my brand new blue and white Oldsmobile. When I entered the store I was engulfed in the beautiful music of Respighi's *Pines of Rome*. I located the source of this music in the record department and Homer introduced me to Maggie Parker, the department head, who was busy unpacking a shipment of records. Maggie was a Minnesota girl with beautiful blonde hair and blue eyes. It was love at first sight, pushed along by the music. I proposed marriage that evening! We were married two and a half months later. We are still married, which confirms the power of music. Maggie and I both loved classical music with a passion and that's what brought us together in a whirlwind courtship and helps keep us together 47 years later.

My parents were distraught. After all the years of their careful coaching: don't marry without a medical examination, meet her parents because that's the way she'll turn out, etc., etc.. All nonsense. And she had a lovely seven-year-old daughter, Brooke, whom I promptly adopted. Maggie introduced me to the works of Gustav Mahler and our home was filled with Mahler's heavenly symphonies (heavy percussion, too) and still is filled with it today.

We had a son the following year whom we named William Frederick Ludwig III; I couldn't wait to pass on my knowledge of drums and drum making.

Buddy Rich Plant Visit

On one of his many trips to and through Chicago, I had Buddy come out to the factory. One day we were both galloping up the stairs to the third floor assembly department, with Buddy taking two steps at a time. I said, "Hey, slow down! You're liable to have a heart attack!" He shot back over his shoulder, "I've got four hearts!" Through the years I really believed that.

In the plant he was very studious about drum manufacturing. He carefully tuned his sets in thirds. He sought perfection and I found having him in the plant helped me indoctrinate my team to use special care in assembling ALL drums! Buddy was a great reinforcement in this respect. All the employees thought so highly of him that they insisted on asking him for his autograph, which pleased him no end.

The Velvet Fog– Mel Torme, Arrives

My brother-in-law, James R. Dodson, who was our sales manager after the war, called from New York. Jim said he had uncovered a fabulous and little known drummer named Mel Torme, and we could get him as an endorser by simply trading him new drums for his old ones. Not being there, I was dubious. Jim hastened to tell me more. This cat was also a crooner. I had to admit I had never heard of him. I held back on the deal, but Jim was persistent and finally admitted that he had already made the deal! I was not happy about it. Shortly thereafter, my father had to let Jim go because of insubordination. That was hard to do. Imagine a father having to dismiss his own daughter's husband from the family business! But Dad had courage– more than I could ever hope to have, I tell you!

When Mel came to Chicago I had to admit that he was a pretty good player, a subsitute for Rich, you might say. But his act was centered around crooning and towards this end he had a tremendous female following. The drumming part of his act was mildly successful. One day I inquired of him why he even bothered with the drumming and he replied, "The girls come to see me with their boyfriends and I know the guys are not too fond of my singing so I thought drumming is a masculine thing and I can capture them as fans also!" Pretty savvy thinking, I thought, and it must have worked because he certainly enjoyed a long and apparently prosperous career. Mel used to arrange dates at the factory and then call the teenage magazines to send a photographer out to the plant. He would arrive in a gold Cadillac convertable full of beautiful fans, all squealing with joy. It was quite a sight in this Polish neighborhood, where a classy car was a three year old Chevy. I had to escort the whole squealing group through the assembly department while Mel arranged corny poses implying that he was making his own set. Cornball. I hated it!

One New Year's Eve I spent on stage at the big Chicago Theatre changing over the hardware from his 26" bass drum to a 24" bass drum, to conform with Rich's latest move. That is where I learned that hole drilling on shells wasn't so precise after all. If it weren't for the ever present rattail file, I never would have completed the assembly in time for the big stroke of twelve curtain opener.

Mel called me often from the road coast to coast every time Buddy changed sizes. He so wanted to be like Buddy! When we made the half-sized set for Buddy to play at the opening of the Shamrock Hotel in Houston, Mel heard about it and called to demand an identical set. I quoted him a thin-air price of $300.00 and he exploded with a string of profanity interlaced with all the good he had done for me on the road. That was our last call. I couldn't take it anymore and hung up. He called back immediately, throwing a threat that he would switch to Slingerland. I said, "Good! Switch!" He did, and Slingerland ran a batch of ads on Mel Torme with his

Slingerland drums to embarass me and to allow Mel to exact a measure of revenge. He never got his half-sized drums, though– ever! Sometimes a fellow can only take so much and then he has to draw a line in the sand.

The Spike Jones Attempted Hold-Up

One day I got a call from the drummer with the famous comedian Spike Jones. I was instantly on alert, since Spike was one of my favorite funnymen. He was hugely popular and playing the week or two at the top venue in town, the Chicago Theater, reportedly for $5,000.00 per week. His drummer said they were looking for several sets of drums, three to be exact, and would like to come out between shows and discuss a deal. I said eagerly, "Come ahead!"

At the appointed time I greeted Spike and his drummer in our office and could hardly contain my excitement. After a hurried factory tour we sat down in the office and he outlined what he wanted; two complete sets in contrasting colors and sizes, plus a "breakaway" set. I said, "Huh?" He explained that a smaller set would be slid out on stage towards the completion of the act which he would play. Then a secret lever would be activated and the set would fall apart. I had been carefully notating his needs but when I got to the breakaway set I said I didn't see how we could do that. The regular two sets could be built in short order for a wholesale price of $900.00. "What!" he exploded. Then he turned to his drummer and said, "See? I *told* you it would do no good coming out here!" With that, they both stormed out of the office and I thought, "good riddance to a couple of bandits!" Subsequently Slingerland made a deal with Spike Jones and wasted money on Spike Jones ads which didn't sell him a single outfit! Sometimes you have to put your foot down!

The Great Crosstown Head Race

Throughout all of the decade of the 1950s, I was in a car and foot race with Bud Slingerland to get the best calf skin heads for our increasing drum production. There were four sources of supply and we would often find ourselves facing one another in the waiting rooms of one of the drum head tanneries. When that happened, which was often, we exchanged fairly civilized greetings, but there was a feeling of triumph in the breast of whoever got there first! The two main suppliers were American Rawhide Manufacturing Company and the White Eagle Rawhide Manufacturing Company. Each would call us both as nearly simultaneously as possible with the news that a fresh supply of calfskin and slunk heads was assembled for our picking and approval. When I got that call I would drop whatever I was doing

and race through the office, coat tails flying, jump into my car and floor it down to that tannery. Arriving ahead of Bud gave me a tremendous feeling of jubilation since I would then go through the stacks of freshly tanned heads picking out only the best and leaving the poorest for Bud. The same happened if Bud won the race. Gretsch came in third since they were preoccupied with guitars and their general jobbing business downtown on Wabash avenue.

Selecting heads involved holding each one up to the light to search for salt stains which would discolor the heads on the drum. Also we held the edges between both hands and passed the head completely around the circumference searching for evenness in thickness. A thin head would be good for snare drums and a thick one for parade drums.

It was at about this time that our sales manager, Fred Miller, changed our nomenclature from "field" drums to "parade" drums as these drums were no longer used on the field but on parade.

Calf heads were tanned from yearling calves less than a year in age. Slunk skins were tanned from unborn calfskins which, as gruesome as it sounds, were often by products of the cow slaughtering process. These slunk skins were also used for many other products such as fine leather men's and ladies' gloves. Since cattle were sold to the slaughter houses by weight, farmers did not hesitate to sell pregnant cows for meat and the unborn calf became a profitable by-product. Naturally the slunk skins were extremely undeveloped and therefore thin and ideal for snare heads. Because of the economy of this process, there were always far more slunk snare drum heads available than calf batter heads. But I had to beware! Very often there were tiny pin holes in the head which could only be discovered by holding the skins up to a light. Slunk skins had to be carefully selected and if Bud was in the waiting room, I took extra care and time to leave him as many pin-holed slunk skins and salt-stained batter heads as possible. He did likewise, thus the "Great Cross Town Races"!

Timpani heads were particularly difficult to choose for the highest quality assuring the performer the very best sound. One professional timpanist in particular , Cloyd Duff of the Cleveland Symphony Orchestra, would order six timpani heads each summer directly from my father who would then begin to go through stacks of timpani heads looking for only the special, special best. When he had six even transparent calf skin heads he would ship them. Duff would then pick out four and return two! This careful head selection made our drums sound better and look better as well. Each drum was tuned to play at the end of the assembly line and then packed for shipment. Every timpano was hand-fitted with the appropriate thickness calf skin head for the particular size timpano by my Dad or me. For instance, the smaller-sized timpani were fitted with thicker heads to provide more body. Otherwise, the small diameter of the kettle would sound thin to the ears. Larger diameters of timpani were fitted with thinner heads to enhance a quicker response to the sticks. You would

Maggie and daughter Brooke wave from the boat I bought shortly after our marriage. We spent many weekends together on the water.

expect larger to be thicker and smaller to be thinner, but no; it was the other way around; larger sizes were thinner than smaller sizes. That was the way it was for the final decade of the calf skin era which, unknown to everyone, was rapidly coming to a close. With the close of that era, a certain competitive advantage would be lost.

Our First Million-Dollar Year!

As if in response to my happy marriage to Maggie Parker, our sales in 1954 soared to the lofty figure of $1,015,178.00, with a profit of $14,866.00. This was the second time in our personal drum making history that sales had exceeded a million dollars, the first being 1928 just before the start of the Great Depression triggered by the stock market crash of October 1929. I was so elated! It was a triumph I carried with me to many a bar!

My drummer-chasing in the night clubs was curtailed by my young marriage, so I began to depend more on a young man I had hired partially for this purpose years before, Dave Arndt. Dave was a number of years younger than me and handled professional calls in a very excited fashion. I began to get more rest being at home every night, and my life became a more natural, orderly existence.

We bought a ranch house in River Forest, just nine miles west of Damen Ave. and the plant. I played in the local symphony orchestra as well as the church orchestra for the High Holy services. Maggie accompanied me on many business trips and proved to be an excellent hostess at many WFL dealer functions. The great-

est decade of drumdom was about to open.

Rumors Of A Drum Company For Sale

As if my marriage to Maggie was an omen of good things to come, the pace of changes in the drum industry introduced me to some startling events. All through the winter of 1954-55, rumors abounded that the C.G.Conn company was interested in selling their entire drum division! Rumors such as these set my imagination running wildly in all directions at once. Foremost in my mind was the chance to recapture my name!

To refresh some history a bit: in 1947 the Conn Corporation decided to merge their two drum divisions in name, just as they had been physically in the factories since 1930. They put the names together, handing us (Ludwig) the ultimate insult, placing the Leedy name before ours. The new company would thus become Leedy & Ludwig. This was the original order of purchase by them, so I guess it made sense. I, nevertheless, thought our name was stronger and therefore should have been first.

Leedy was founded earlier than Ludwig in 1895. Ulysses Grant Leedy was a drummer in the old Orpheum Theatre on Monument Circle in downtown Indianapolis. He was christened after the famous Civil War hero, Ulysses S. Grant, the general who led the Union forces to victory in 1865. U. G. Leedy must have been a most energetic drummer for he not only played the drums but built and operated a hundred contraptions (later shortened to "traps") providing sound to the silent pictures of that era: rooster calls, lion roars, steam locomotives, etc. In addition to the movies shown in theaters of the day, a live vaudeville show with four or five acts was presented to give the projectionist time to re-wind the feature film and newsreel by hand for the next show. Even more sound effects (such as gunshots and horses hooves) were needed to properly accompany the live acts. To allow the drummer a rest break, an organist would play singalong songs during which the audience followed a bouncing ball from one word to the next in perfect synchronization with the organist. These two hour shows were repeated four or five times per day. Mr. Leedy reported for work at around noon and didn't finish until ten at night! He was, indeed, an iron man and early pictures of him show a big, robust fellow.

Since manufacturing was in its infancy at the time, Mr. Leedy had to make up many of his own sound effects. Drummers saw them and heard about Mr. Leedy and, like my father twenty years later, he suddenly found himself in the drum manufacturing business. U. G. Leedy had two sons, neither of whom expressed a keen desire to work in the percussion industry. In fact, Mr. Leedy had to discharge one of them when he caught him napping in a quiet corner of the plant.

The Leedy Company excelled in the production of mallet percussion instruments as well, while Ludwig & Ludwig found it easier to "job" their mallet instrument line from J.C.Deagan Company in Chicago.

Like Ludwig & Ludwig, Leedy's company had been stressed by heavy investments in banjo production. Business was further hurt by the advent of sound pictures. Those factors along with Mr. Leedy's failing health prompted him to sell his business to Conn in 1929.

During World War II, the Conn corporation was a major player in the development of radar and other electronic products. They had an ability to form brass tubing in a seamless configuration that won them many lucrative contracts for essential war work. At the end of the war, the owners (the Greenleaf family) looked for civilian products which could be manufactured with the wartime expertise Conn had developed. They came up with the idea of making electronic organs. (The leader in the field at that time was the Hammond Organ Company.)

For the next ten years, Conn concentrated their efforts and capital on the vast, expensive tooling required to produce electronic organs in all sizes and prices to meet the Hammond competition. Finally by 1954, they were producing four models. The trade demanded a fifth model, a spinet organ which would require an additional $350,000 in capital. Being already heavily in debt to local banks, Conn received an ultimatum; sell off some divisions or no further loans!

Conn at the time owned the main hotel (the Hotel Elkhart), the local newspaper (*The Elkhart Truth*), four grain elevators, a wholesale operation called Continental Music Company headquartered in Evanston, Illinois, and two drum companies which they had combined into one, Leedy & Ludwig. Mr. Lee Greenleaf, a son of the Conn President C. D. Greenleaf, told me he had been in the drum division factory only twice in twenty five years. Drums were the least attractive as well as least profitable division in the whole conglomorate, so the division was put up for sale in the spring of 1955.

We Make A Small Acquisition

I pestered my father to death on at least acquiring our instruction book library, which included all of the Ludwig & Ludwig drum corps instruction books of the 1920s. He refused to consider it, saying we were doing all right with our W.F.L. methods and not to "rock the boat." "But Dad," I replied, "We get to use the Ludwig name on these books!" Finally he relented when I got Conn's price down to $12,000 for the six books including the Moeller book. We sent the check and they sent the printing plates. Upon completion of the deal (my first), I resolved to purchase at least my name and restore it to its rightful owners–us! But doing that in the face of my father's stern opposition stymied me.

Mr. Paul Gazly, a vice president of Conn, had been designated as the seller of the drum division. He lived in Evanston, Illinois, and spent his Mondays at the Continental office on Ridge Road in Evanston, spent Tuesday through Thursday down in Elkhart, Indiana, at the Conn Plant, and finished out the week back in Evanston at the Continental Wholesale operation. I called him often on Mondays and Fridays at the Continental location and monitored his progress in selling off the drum division.

I knew before the press releases when he sold the entire inventory of finished goods to a wholesaler in Newark, N.J., Dorn & Kirschner. Next to be "spun off" was the mallet division, which was sold to the Jenkins Company in Decator, Illinois. The owner of Jenkins was Grover Jenkins, who concentrated on manufacturing very low-cost percussion instruments of questionable quality. Grover once asked me to guess why we (the U.S.A.) were having so much trouble with the Russians. His answer? He had sold them three sets of his timpani! (Big laughter!)

Still, no one had expressed any interest in the names Leedy or Ludwig or the machinery and tools and dies! At this point, my father and mother announced their plans to motor to Florida for a couple of weeks rest at Key Biscayne, as they had in prior years. I greeted this announcement with joy, for it would give me an opportunity to put my plan into operation the minute they cleared Chicago's city limits.

Well, Bud, How About It?

I put in a call to Bud Slingerland and proposed a meeting in his office which he viewed with suspicion. He declined, so I suggested my office. Again he declined, wanting to know why we couldn't discuss whatever I had called about over the phone. "O.K., Bud," I replied, and took a deep breath. "How about you and I splitting up Leedy & Ludwig right down the middle? Gazly has the price down to around $200,000.00 and no takers. I think if we jointly offer $95,000 each for a total of $190,000, he'll take it." Bud Slingerland was slow to respond, as he always was, so I described how he could make the Leedy line in his plant right along with his regular Slingerland line, and have the Leedy timpani line as well. I believe that tipped him in my direction because later that day he called his approval and I set a date to meet Paul Gazly with him the next Friday. That meeting lasted just two hours and we had a deal on a handshake. Now where would I find $90,000?

That night I called my father and addressed him as Mr. President of Ludwig & Ludwig and he was very confused. Then I happily told him what I had done and we had our name back. Instead of joining me enthusiastically, he was furious and berated me for the better part of ten minutes. How I suffered! But nothing could dampen my enthusiasm; I had my name back. The next day I announced the development to my staff and began calling leading dealers. I was very happy, and basked in their enthusiastic congratulations.

We got Our Name Back!

On Mar. 4, 1955 we, (WFL Drum Co.) bought our name "LUDWIG" from C. G. CONN LTD. including Publications, machinery, tools, dies, etc., and the complete LUDWIG TYMPANI department.

Where do we go from here?

1 We will service all former L & L dealers and their repair problems.
2 Every popular model from the former L & L Line will be incorporated into the WFL Drum production schedule.
3 We are changing our name to **LUDWIG DRUM CO.** and will continue the manufacture of the entire WFL Drum line.

All of us here, at WFL thank you for making this change possible. We assure you of our interest and hope to serve you promptly in the future.

LUDWIG DRUM CO.

Makers: WFL Drum Line

1728 N. DAMEN AVE. • CHICAGO 47, ILLINOIS

Then followed a complicated sales contract from Conn's attorneys, a bank loan, and finally a contract-signing in Gazly's office, all within one week. At one of those meetings I asked Bud what was his deciding factor in approving the 50/50 deal and he replied, "I figure the No. 1 dealer in every town will have the Slingerland line and the No. 2 dealer will have my new rebuilt Leedy line." I thought, but didn't say, "In a pigs ear, guy."

The next sixteen weeks were filled with grueling trips to Elkhart on Tuesdays to Thursdays, separating the machinery, tooling, patents, advertising and arranging with the local trucking firm to haul it all out Fridays to arrive at our plant each Monday. My father grudgingly took part in these Elkhart meetings as he knew a lot of the tooling from his Ludwig & Ludwig days. Most of the time we rode the New York Central train down and back since Elkhart was an important division point in the New York Central system. Sometimes Bud would be on the train and we would chat amiably. I found him to be well educated and a genuinely pleasant fellow after all.

In 1955 the Ludwig Company unveiled its first large prefabricated convention display with recessed spotlights and built-in stick and beater displays. All the sales personnel were uniformed, and prominent drummers were featured in hourly demonstrations.

Gradually the gruffness we had towards each other wore down a little. When we couldn't identify a die set or part of a tooling, we had to rely on the Conn engineers to come over to the ex-drum works to help us out.

A particularly lengthy problem arose in assembling all of the timpani dies in order of use in production. That alone took days, but I couldn't blame Bud since he was going to put them in production to replace his broken down, poorly engineered and designed timpani line.

We gradually changed our advertising, including catalogs, over to Ludwig Drum Co. where it is to this day.

A Government Order For 24 Pairs of Timpani

A bid invitation arrived for twenty four pedal tuned timpani, copper bowls with trunks. Knowing Slingerland's previous price on the big order for 200 pairs, I worked hard to come up with a price that would beat his. I recalled that once while roaming the H.N. White plant in Cleveland when my dad was working there I had come across a large inventory of trunk latches that had been used in building Sousaphone trunks. Business was slow on those trunks, so the latches had piled up through the years. I put in a call to Ernie Long, the foreman, and he assured me they had enough for 24 timpani trunk sets. I thought, "this is a place I can save some money." I received a special low price on these latches and hinges and won the bid from the government on the 24 pairs of timps. The trunks were shipped to us from the White plant in Cleveland, and we packed

the timpani in them. We shipped them out, and sent our bill to the quartermaster department in Philadelphia. Soon after, we received an irate call from a very nasty Earl Cochran that the trunks were not the equal of the Schussler-made Taylor type of trunk. (The only difference was that the Schussler trunks were covered with fiber outside while the White trunks were heavy duty olive drab covered.) An argument ensued but I could not budge Cochran, so I ended the conversation promising to come to Philadelphia the following week and bring along Mr. Long, the foreman at White's under whose supervision the trunks had been manufactured. Ernie Long had never been in an airplane but agreed to accompany me. I assured him we would have a smooth two-hour ride over the Alleghany Mountains into Philadelphia. The next week I flew from Chicago to Cleveland, where Ernie boarded the flight which continued to Philadelphia.

Riders Of The Sky

Very soon after takeoff dinner was served, and just as soon, dinner was all over us. We encountered a gigantic storm over the mountains and both Ernie and I turned absolutely white with fright. This was the day of non-pressurized cabins, so the maximum altitude of that aircraft was only 10,000 feet! That meant they flew *through* storms instead of over them. There were some quiet spots during which Ernie hauled out a pocket full of family pictures as if viewing them for the last time. It was the roughest airplane ride I ever had. When it was time to leave Philadelphia, Ernie took the train home and to my knowledge never ventured from the earth again!

Arguing With The Government

The next morning we arrived at the Quartermaster Department at the appointed time. It was the same building where just a few years before I had appeared before the general committee to be released from the sling award. I wondered if I would be as lucky this time.

Cochran showed us a large room where all 48 trunks and timpani were lined up with lids up at attention in Army style! We went down the line inspecting each individual trunk with Ernie Long agreeing with Cochrane that there were indeed rust spots showing on some of the latches and hinges for the corners. I could have killed him! We had agreed, I thought, that we would together reject Cochran's claims of inferior workmanship. Cochran maintained that I knew the type of trunks they wanted which were the Schussler Taylor-type trunks. I maintained just as stoutly that what we supplied was just as good and that there were no specifications for timpani trunks. We argued back and forth for the better part of the morning and Ernie was no help at all. Finally I caved in and asked if they would be willing to return the cases *to the White plant* for a rust preventive coating, and to this, Cochran agreed. I stipulated that they were to send back only the trunks; they were to hold the timpani there. Two weeks later, a frantic Ernie Long called from Cleveland saying 6,500 lbs. of trunks had arrived at the New York Central depot in downtown Cleveland. They were all still loaded with the timpani. There went my profit on the deal right there. The management of the White Co. refused to accept them and forwarded the entire shipment to W.F.L. Drum Co. on Damen Ave. It was hell, I tell you. We took them all back and applied the preventive coating ourselves including all of each trunk and sent them back to the Philadelphia Quartermaster Department *prepaid*! We lost heavily on that deal, not to mention the heck of a rough airplane ride that scared Mr. Long to death. Of such are the fickle forces of destiny! Lesson No. 578: never, never argue with the United States Government!!

A Marketing Manager Comes Aboard

One summer day, a student at Northwestern's School of Music called up for an appointment. At the appointed time a very young Dick Schory walked into my office and I showed him around our expanding plant. He was visibly impressed. Shortly thereafter, he applied for a summer position on my staff and there was something quite charismatic about this young man, so I invited him to join us for summers. I taught him how to run the addressograph and had him running the daily post to the post office, and other little jobs like that which freed me for other tasks. Each summer, for I think two summers, I could rely on young Dick to come into the office and help out. Though he had studied to become a band director and could look forward to immediate employment upon graduation, I met his request for a ten year promise of an annual salary increase the same as he was offered in academia. It proved to be a wise decision—one of my best. Through the years that followed, Dick Schory rose to be my marketing manager.

And a market builder he was! He pointed us into the direction of total percussion by including the Musser line in our catalogs. He saw the potential of percussion

Dick Schory   Master Market Builder

ensembles in building a market for total percussion. He hired friends in the percussion world to compose percussion ensemble pieces at the high school level and published them himself, selling them to the company as needed. The purpose was to create a market for marimbas, xylophones, bells, chimes, and all else in the percussion world which previously sold in very limited quantities. Dick Schory saw the potential of percussion expansion and aggressively pursued it. He sent various mallet instruments to band composers such as Vaclav Nelhybel, for instance, so they could set these up in their studios and learn the range, tonal sonorities, and possibilities of each instrument.

At the end of the ten years, Schory's income was far

Pep with Clair Musser

F.K. Peppler drilling members of the road crew on the nuances of positive percussion

F.K. "Pep" Peppler

higher than planned due to his fantastic energy. Dick went on to organize his own percussion ensemble, arranging for us to supply the instruments. He made many exciting recordings which further spread the appeal of percussion instruments to the public at large. He turned out to be a true director of marketing– someone who *built* markets rather than just seeing that the company's products were placed before the buying public. Today's percussion suppliers owe Dick Schory a debt of gratitude!

Another good personnel choice I made was for the position of sales manager, F.K. "Pep" Peppler. The reader will recall that I referred to Pep earlier in this narrative as a traveling companion in the days before the war when we were both youngsters fresh to the road. Prior to entering the service, Pep had been working for the Deagan Company. Pep served with great distinction throughout the war as an artillery officer in the Italian campaign. At the end of the war there was a major campaign encouraging all Americans to welcome back the soldiers who had so bravely defended our way of life. To a large extent, this campaign was aimed at employers who were encouraged to rehire former employees to pick up where they left off. Jack Deagan, the inherited head of the J.C. Deagan company after World War II, did not heed those suggestions. Enjoying the postwar business boom, Jack felt there was no longer a need for salesmen, so he refused to hire Pep back. (This was a factor in Clair Musser deciding to leave Deagan and start the Musser Company.) I gladly hired Pep; he was a welcome and experienced addition to my staff and he stayed until his premature death. He rose in my organization to be a Vice-President, as did Dick Schory. Pepler organized our extensive thirteen-man sales force over the years and appointed Dick Gerlach as sales manager in his place when he, Pep, was promoted. Dick Gerlach stayed with the company a record 41 years, from 1960 to 2001!

The 1957 Catalog

The 1957 catalog cover featured a montage of all the markets we were engaged in. It was very colorful. On the first page inside the cover was a picture of the factory followed by an illustration of the staff with the father and son team William F. Ludwig Sr. and Jr. at the top. This catalog featured Buddy Rich and a duplicate of his marine pearl outfit including the low-mount shell-mount ride cymbal holder.

A feature of this catalog was the introduction of the

Ludwig's first drum kit. The cardboard box was not very durable and was soon replaced with a fiber case. A record of the thirteen essential drum rudiments was included. The author's daughter, Brooke, sat in for this catalog shot.

first snare drum kit. When Dick Schory first brought up the idea of a case with a snare drum, stand, sticks, book, and pad, we were not sure whether it would sell. Dick put together a prototype kit and took it to Marion Karnes of Karnes Music. Marion placed a large order for the kits, recognizing that he could rent it to beginners during his recruitment drives along with all the other instruments that were already being rented. Marion Karnes was one of Chicagoland's most enterprising dealers, and the tremendous success of the snare drum kit is a fitting legacy to both he and Dick Schory. (Karnes Music is still a thriving multistore operation in Chicagoland, though Marion Karnes died in the early 1990s.)

I continued to add name drummers to our "stable" of stars. Among them were Jo Jones, Ray McKinley, and Ed Thigpen. Problems continued with my "tiger," Buddy Rich.

Enter Joe The Great

On one of my many trips to New York City I met the

fabulous jazz pianist, Marion McPartland. She was performing nightly with her own trio at the Hickory House Bar. Her drummer was Mousie Alexander who blended in so well it seemed like they were meant for each other. And Mousie already had Ludwig drums! It was with some surprise that I picked up the phone months later to hear from Marion that she had changed drummers and this one I should come down to the "Down Beat" club to meet. His name was Joe Morello. I did go, and Joe had a problem with his Speed King pedal. He also had a sparkling silver finish Ludwig set. I attended to the repair of his pedal on.the spot and that was the beginning of one of the greatest friendships I have ever had in drumdom. It continues to this day. We became inseparable. With his fast wit and sunny disposition, Joe was completely the opposite of Rich. And his technique was almighty.

Posing after another highly successful Joe Morello clinic at Eighth Street Music in Philadelphia: the author, Dick Schory, Joe Morello, and Gary Burton.

Joe Morello's clinics were always sensational in terms of content and technique, although I did find it neccessary to help him develop his presentation skills such as repeating audience questions so everyone knew what he was talking about, and not getting sidetracked.

Joe will never forget the time I stopped by his hotel around supper time and asked to borrow his shower. He claims I stepped out without clothes. I claim I had a towel. Whichever, if you have the pleasure of knowing Joe Morello he'll give you his version with gusto. Later, Joe left the Marion McPartland Trio to join the Dave Brubeck Quartet, where his fame rose mightily. And he was a great clinician too. Finally, my cup runneth over! He was just a natural teacher, even though severely handicapped since birth by near blindness. He memorized every arrangement and never missed a beat. He was born to drum! He loved to play chess as I do and he gave me a set with extra large pieces and an over-sized board to help him with his limited eyesight. We loved nothing in life better than playing all night after his job with Brubeck, ending at dawn in a kitchen full of empty beer cans! We were evenly matched, too, which made it all the more enjoyable. Those games and days are gone, but I'll nurture those beautiful memories for-

ever. He was not only a wonderful percussionist but a great loving human being as well. I miss seeing him.

Time For Another Building

We were again bursting at the seams. Acquiring the Ludwig name brought us a flood of new business and I had the feeling we were not only gaining on Bud Slingerland but had perhaps even surpassed him! Sales for 1957 came in at $2,364,000 with net profit at $125,000, or 5%. Seeing no problems on the horizon, I called for another 10,000 square foot expansion to the Damen Ave. facility. This latest three-floor expansion fronted on Damen Avenue. The new high-ceiling basement accomodated an en-

The 1958 10,000 sq ft expansion is circled in the top photo. In the middle of this construction, the city of Chicago condemned the Damen Avenue frontage of the original building which was starting to bulge out. It had to be replaced at a cost of $32,000.00. The bottom photo shows both completed construction projects.

larged punch press department plus added two floors above. We gained new office space on the first floor.

Mystery Orders Arrive

In the spring of 1958, we received a very unusual order from one Marion "Chick" Evans of Santa Fe, New Mexico, for 144 assorted wooden flesh hoops. This was extremely unusual and we asked Evans what they were for. He replied he was experimenting with a new material to replace calf skin heads. This idea was not new to us because through the years we had experimented with "doping" calf skin heads to weather-proof them. I was curious, so I filled the order for the gross of flesh hoops. Then Joe Grolimund, president of the Selmer Company, sent in an order for several dozen flesh hoops. This was my introduction to the mighty plastic head era. Both Grolimund and Evans sent us the first Mylar heads we had ever seen *tacked*... yes, stapled to our wood hoops. They were indeed weatherproof and performed well on a drum *if* you didn't over tighten the heads. When this happened, the mylar simply pulled away from the flesh hoop.

We at first dismissed the idea of replacing calf skin heads as just another aborted attempt at "weatherproofing" heads. When I told Howard Emory, the genial head of American Rawhide and our principal supplier of quality skin heads about mylar, he looked up at me from his desk and quizzically asked, "Should I sell my tannery?"

We all now know that is exactly what he should have done, for it was not long before Remo and Ludwig developed ways of securing the mylar into aluminum channeled hoops so they would not pull out. One day I came across my father in his office bending the long leg of a channeled aluminum hoop over an inner hoop between the two, holding a mylar head with plyers! He was one to get around the other fellow's ideas if he could and thus was born another method of mounting the slippery mylar so it would not pull out under tension. We secured a patent on this idea which was immediately copied by Bud Slingerland. We sued in patent court for protection, but after a week's trial, we lost. We also lost $180,000 in the process, and our idea became common property of the industry and widely copied to this day. Even such export driven countries as Korea, Taiwan, and, yes, mainland China, now supply mylar heads mounted on our design of interlocking hoops. Some history about mylar: during World War II the British RAF planes were constantly plagued by the cellophane film breaking in movie cameras. The War Department requested scientists exercise an all-out effort to create a movie film which would be impervious to heat, cold, and changes in temperatures especially in reconnaissance flights over possible targets. Scientists came up with mylar movie film. One of the largest producers of mylar is the Du Pont Chemical company which aggressively sought post-war markets for their proud new product. In the musical instrument field, the ever alert Joe Grolimund switched the saxophone pad production over to mylar because of its moisture resistant qualities. Since Joe had once worked for my Dad in the old Ludwig & Ludwig company, he quickly sought to adopt mylar to drum heads. The samples Joe sent us were too thin and pulled off the hoops. Our new patent "crimping" method illustrated here solved that and will be around in the industry for a good long time.

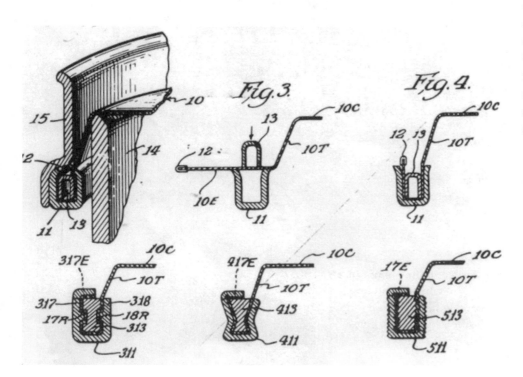

With ground breaking innovations like this, the drum world was beginning to notice the Ludwig Drum Company. We built a stand-alone two story brick building on two cleared lots behind us and across the alley, just for manufacturing mylar heads. We designed and built ourselves twenty four high compression presses which both heated and formed the mylar into drum heads in all sizes. At our peak, we were turning out 3,000 heads every day. Naturally our purchases of calf skin heads became less and less until one day Howard Emory of Amrawco paid us a visit. He and his brother were in tears at what they saw. Literally the death knell of an entire one thousand year industry. But, hey, that's progress!

I was overjoyed! Gone were the days of racing across town to beat Bud Slingerland to the tanneries. Gone, the heavy shoulder-trucking of tightly rolled heads carried like rifles on my young shoulders. And, yes, gone, the endless scanning every one for pin holes and salt stains before accepting each and every head. BUT... and this is a big, big BUT– we lost our selectivity; our advantage of providing a personal selection of heads for our customers. As I began to realize this, my joy became short lived. Mylar provided strong, weather proof heads but they were all even in thickness and exactly alike and drums started to sound alike too! Today head manufacturers make stacks of heads every day, something like flap jacks. The ability to fill our own drum head needs within the confines of the Damen Avenue facility was a great boon to our production. I find it interesting now to muse—we, a drum company made drum heads for our drums. Remo started out making heads only and later got into drum manufacture to use some of his production of mylar drum heads.

Construction of (top) and completed (bottom) Willow Street 10,000 square foot mylar drum head plant. Note the miniature elevator shaft. The fully electric elevator was exactly half the size of a regular elevator and was used for outside raw material delivery.

As the dozen or so drum head suppliers continue to bring out new versions of mylar adaptations, some of the old line tanneries hang on. United Rawhide is the principal tanner left in the United States. Stephen Palansky is the genial proprietor and he welcomes any and all requests for genuine high quality calf skin heads which come his way. There are several foreign tanneries as well — Ireland is home to the famous Vellum & Parchment Works. There is a tannery in southern England, and a large one in eastern Germany that provides an incredible range of animal hides; goat, calf, horse, etc.

I have in my possession two "long" drums which are replicas of the long drums of the Revolutionary War 227 years ago. The shells are 20" deep and 17" in diameter, made by the famous Eastern drum maker Cooperman Drum Co. in Connecticut with loving care by just a five man work force. Their sawmill is in Vermont so you know the wood is prime virgin birch and maple. One of my long drums is equipped with calf heads and the other mylar heads. Both drums are strung with thick gut snares clamped rather tightly to the snare head. Both really roar when I open up. But the calf head drum steadily loses its snap and pitch in damp weather while the mylar equipped drum stays up and provides constant and steady response. When I give my "History.of Percussion" lecture, guess which drum travels with me?

Back to the early days of mylar heads introduced in 1957. There was considerable skepticism amongst the die-hard professional percussionists such as the late John Noonan of Bloomington, Illinois, who wrote: "How dare you take it upon yourselves (Ludwig Drum Co.) to switch drum orders from calf skin to mylar heads without the customer's approval!" To John and others like him I

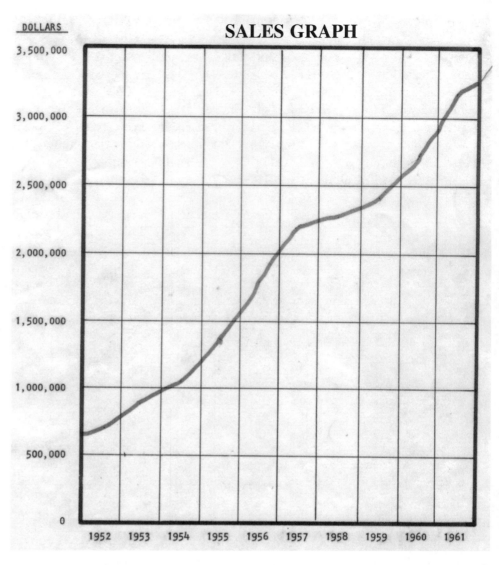

SALES GRAPH

Graphing always helped me visualize where we were and where we were going.

could only say we did it in what we thought was the best interest of the customers. In fact, at one drum and bugle corps contest sponsored by the American Legion, I strapped on my Ludwig 12" x 15" parade drum and marched across the field from goal post to goal post— 120 yards in a drenching downpour which had stopped that competition dead in its tracks. Judges cowering under the tarps said, "Look at that fool marching solo across the field. He'll ruin that drum!" Of course nothing like that ever happened. I made such a favorable impression that I personally staged other demonstrations. One in particular I recall occured at a Los Angeles drum show. I had obtained the plastic nose cone from a discarded B24 bomber and filled it with water. At the high point of my demo, I would drop one of our best and most expensive snare drums into the transparent cone and the drum would float. Then I removed it, wiped it off and played upon it and that drum responded as if the

incident had never happened! To demonstrate strength, I would then place that same snare drum on the floor, and from a height of four feet, drop a 16 lb. bowling ball (mine) directly dead center and that ball would bounce right back into my waiting arms. That head did not break. The audience was awed every time. But the head was dished, which I removed by applying heat with a hair curler. Removing knicks and dents with a heater is something still done today. Others, I am sure, demonstrated the advantages of mylar drum heads over calfskin but that was the way I did it. And I took that act coast to coast and many old timers will remember it. Slowly, mylar caught on and now some forty years later, new generations of drummers never played on or even saw a calf skin drum head !

Forever after, we were never out of heads for drum production!

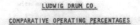

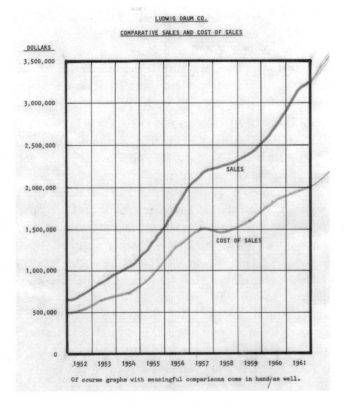

LUDWIG DRUM CO.
COMPARATIVE SALES AND COST OF SALES

Of course graphs with meaningful comparisons come in handy as well.

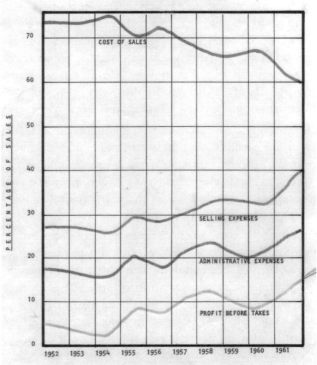

LUDWIG DRUM CO.
COMPARATIVE OPERATING PERCENTAGES

The lower three lines must never cross! The top line is added
to indicate a helpful sign--lowering costs of sales and manufacturing.

Graphing was taught in the economics course I took at the University of Illinois. I had our certified public accountant, Mr. Seybold, prepare a series of graphs to give me a better understanding of our progress. Here are four of these graphs and since sales alone don't mean much, I have included comparative graphs which economists point out should never indicate crossing lines. If any of these lines cross, you are in trouble!

Drum Corps Embrace Mylar Heads

Of all drummers taking advantage of the new mylar heads, none surpassed the marching drummer units. Whether they be drum and bugle corps or marching football bands, they needed the weather protection the most. For these people, we invested in heavy ply mylar and eventually two sheets glued together in what quickly became known as laminated mylar "parade" heads. And what a boon they were! While the rest of the drumming fraternity hesitated, the marching bands and corps changed over in a big way. Good sounding crisp parade drums helped corps win points and victories in competition. Being the inventor of the rolled crimping clamping method, our corps began winning contests over the Slingerland corps. Slingerland was our only competitor in the marching field. Since mylar was so impervious to weather, they never shrank and curled on the flesh hoop and thus marching units could carry piles of heads ready to mount on their drums in case of accidents. One par-

P-127B

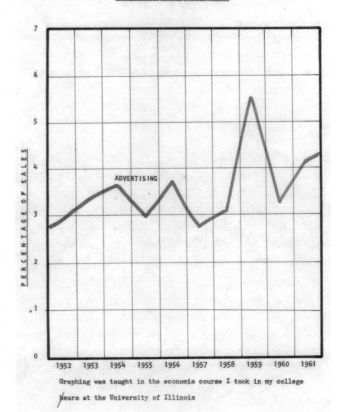

LUDWIG DRUM CO.
RATIO OF
ADVERTISING EXPENSES TO SALES

Graphing was taught in the economis course I took in my college
years at the University of Illinois

ticularly alert drum corps dealer set up his own drum corps specialist organization– Smith Music Sales. This enterprising young man, Glenn C. Smith, was an accomplished brass player and was able to communicate fully with the drum corps as to their needs. He also stocked bugles and drums and spare parts and appeared in his own van at all the important competition events sponsored by the American Legion and later the V.F.W.. The Seniors of this last organization set up special rules admitting Juniors— those under 21 years of age. It was a very lively and competitive outfit and I joined "Smitty" as he was called, in many field competitions, selling Ludwig against Slingerland. My experiences competing against Slingerland in the marching field date back to 1932 where at an Illinois State competition held in Rockford, Illinois, I found Ludwig & Ludwig drums with Slingerland logos. In reporting this to my Dad, he was as furious as I had ever seen him unless I messed up a rudiment during my childhood practice pad years. In tracking down this oddity, we found that the Slingerland sales manager, Sam Rowland, had offered to refinish drums in the Chicagoland area. Obviously Slingerland had no Ludwig badges to install on the re-finished drums, so they installed Slingerland badges. Suddenly all the corps in our area were blossoming with Slingerland logos! I believe this was my first exposure to Slingerland treachery which was to consume me for a lifetime. Drums in those days were lacquer painted,so could be re-finished with ease. This was Slingerland's first attempt to gain recognition in the marching field. Thus my fighting stance latter was tireless and bitter with the assistance of Smith Music Sales. Eventually we were able to point with pride at the 1960 nationals that eleven of the twelve finalists in that competition were Ludwig equipped. The winner carried Slingerland. Sometimes you just can't get it right !

The Glory Years Opened In 1960

In 1960 we came up with $2,900.000 in sales and in 1961 sales reached $3,206,915 producing a net profit of $204,090 (6.36 %). The significance of these figures is that sales were steadily increasing at approximately 13% per year and profitability as well.

It was time for another building. This time a real monster. To the north of our main plant, an old factory building stood on the corner of Damen Ave. and Willow Street. The owner, Saul Applebaum, wanted $100,000 for it. My father refused saying, "I know what he paid for it — $18,000 !"

The Kay Guitar Company was one of the six plants in our Union group and had invested in a new state-of-the-art factory built to their design from the ground up.

I told Dad about it and urged that we take a look at the finished product. It was truly magnificent, sitting on a railroad siding for easy delivery of masses of wood panels used for guitar manufacture. And it was all on one floor– no floor load problems here! And no elevators, of which we had three. On the road back to our plant I tested Dad to move as Kay had done. As we turned the corner of Damen and Willow, he said, "Nothing doing. If you want that kind of a plant you move out there and start your own drum company." I thought this was a cruel response because as it turned out that was exactly the move which should have been made at that time— 1960. So it was with heavy heart that I returned to the old practice of acting against my father's wishes which always pained me very much. I called in a new architect to design a building which would take us all the way to the corner — 40,000 new square feet. A year later I offered Applebaum the $100,000 and the deal was done. It proved the right move because in England a tremendous event was about to unfold– the Beatles would get their act together and conquer the rock and roll world!

My Tiger Leaves Us

The incredible news came over the phone from Atlanta — Buddy Rich suffers heart attack! The Great One's heart protested his high tension life and decided to object. I heard the news from a local dealer that Buddy suffered the attack while leading his quartet. He was rushed to New York by special train—air travel was not yet universal and available. There, surgeons repaired the damage but ordered two months of recuperation. It was during that time that Henry Grossman, owner of the Cleveland, Ohio, wholesale music company of the same name and new owner of Rogers Drum Co. contacted Buddy. The offer of $10,000 as an endorsement fee was made through Ellis Tollin of the Philadelphia music store Tollin & Welch. This was the very first payola in the drum industry as far as I know. Fortunately Joe Morello was in the ascendancy in a big way with the Dave Brubeck quartet. He was even written up in *Newsweek* magazine.

The Old World Reaches Out To The New

Foreign distributors were appearing at our trade shows in ever greater numbers. We were not set up to export our products. Up until 1960 our office manager, Mr. Carl Ganier, would routinely file orders from abroad which went unfilled since we were getting pretty well loaded up with our domestic business. My father loved to quote: "We'll take care of the American market and those across the pond will take care of their markets." Still, in spite of ourselves, the pressure continued to build to export our products. Responding to this pressure, we hired a multi-linguist of European background, Mr. Henry Gilbert, to travel "over there" and see what he could sell. He also set up and managed our first display at the Frankfurt, Germany, Messe (fair). Henry brought back a suitcase full of orders from those countries which alerted me to world selling. We needed an export forwarding company in the loop to handle the sometimes complicated paperwork which always accompanies shipments out of our country. We found one whose young German employee handled our documents for two years before leaving that firm to join us. His name was Frank Baxpehler and he became our export manager.

The author (right) with Gotthold Meyer of Germany, who became Ludwig's largest European distributor.

I always felt that a key to our success in the European market was my lovely wife Maggie, shown here in Nuremburg, Germany. For many years Maggie (with the help of Frank Baxpehler's wife Hildegard) organized elegant dinner receptions for distributors at the Frankfurt trade shows. I could not have asked for a better hostess at meetings for distributors; their love of her natural charisma and charm was expressed by their Ludwig brand loyalty. (This was true for domestic distributors as well.)

The early 60s were busy indeed. Frank and I flew to the British trade fair where I met our new distributor, Ivor Arbiter. He was both wholesaler and retailer. His retail shop in central London was called Drum City. They featured all lines including Gretsch and Trixon, the German manufacturer. Gerry Evans was the manager and a real hustler. When the Beatles manager, Brian Epstein, brought Ringo into the shop for a new set (kit over there), he had been using Premier drums made in England, and that's what he wanted his new set to be. It so happened that our pearl plastic salesman had given me a sample of a new black finish which I had named "Oyster Pearl" for lack of a better name. Ringo spotted this on Arbiter's desk and announced that he wanted it on his new set. Ivor explained it was available only on Ludwig and Ringo responded alright, he would have the Ludwig set. Many people have asked through the years how Ringo got on to our drums and that is the story. Next, Ringo wanted our name on the front head so all his friends could see he was big enough to play a foreign set made in America. Then Brian Epstein objected unless Arbiter got the Beatles name on the head also. Ivor could see a possible controversy developing so he sketched the Beatles logo roughly and the head painter put it on that first head. The most famous logo in the rock and roll realm was born to save a drum sale. Ivor worked out a drum for drum trade with Brian and later Gerry Evans sold Ringo's old set for $190. When I visited Ivor and heard the story, I wasn't particularly excited since the Beatles group was just one of many in England at that time. Much later when the Beatles came to America and appeared on the Ed Sullivan show, the enormity of that little transaction in Ivor Arbiter's office began to sink in. The popularity of oyster pearl had us and our plastic supplier scrambling to keep up with the avalanche of orders that kept us back ordered for three and a half years. What irony! After spending half my life in smoking dens begging drummers to play my products, the biggest lands at my door.

In 1961 I resumed publication of the *Ludwig Drummer* magazine last published by the old company in 1929. Dick Schory had a large part in selecting and organiz-

ing the material. Dick also did a lot of work on the new catalogs which were published every other year. His double-page photos of every instrument in the Ludwig and Musser product lines were really impressive. Our convention displays had grown to seventy feet in width. We were using Joe Morello at a dozen big drum clinics per year. I returned to Great Britain, this time with my family: wife Maggie, daughter Brooke, and son Bill III. We rented a car and drove north calling on dealers along the way and thus reinforcing Arbiter's efforts in our behalf. We went both ways by ship. And all three bands aboard featured our drums!

A Final TussleWithThe Quartermaster Department
Word reached me that my old friend at the Philadelphia Quartermaster Depot, Earl Cochran, had retired and was replaced by Florence Walker. I had to meet her as soon as possible if I was to be kept informed of future proposals purchasing drums. I flew there and met Ms. Walker and invited her to dinner at Bookbinders, the famous seafood restaurant. Things were proceeding smoothly enough when a hulk of a man wearing the uniform of the merchant marine began to make his presence known as a captain of a ship in the harbor. We were invited to be his guests, so we took a cab together to the sprawling docks of Philadelphia and boarded his ocean-going freighter which he explained was in the African run. We climbed the atrium type ladder four or five decks and were led into the bridge. The array of sea-going instruments and navigation equipment enthralled me. I got lost pouring over the sea charts and equipment when suddenly a scream snapped me out of my reverie. It came from one side of the bridge behind a closed door. Instantly, I knew Florence was in some kind of trouble since the Captain was not in view either. I rushed to the door, opened it, and was shocked by the horrible sight. That Captain was on top of Florence! Without thinking about it, I rushed to the bunk. I shoved the Captain off with such violence that he rolled between the bunk and the bulkhead where it appeared he was stuck fast. I grabbed Florence's hand and yelled, "RUN!" and we took off following the return route down the atrium steel ladder, fearing being blocked at any second. I recognized the entrance and flew down the outer ladder with Florence close behind. We hit the dock running. and did not stop until we were on land. It was very early in the morning as I searched in vain for a cab– or any moving vehicle or person. Far away in the distance I spotted a man. Florence and I walked towards him. He was standing under a lone streetlight holding his hands in   front. As we got closer, I could see that he was urinating. I turned to block this obnoxious view from

Florence and we headed in a new direction. Finally a taxi drove into view and I got Florence home. I returned to my hotel and collapsed into bed.

The next day I called Florence and she seemed none the worse for our mad dash earlier that morning to escape the drunken Captain. I asked for an appointment and she invited me out. I wanted to look up some things in the repair department. When we walked through, I recognized a pair of timpani trunks as Slingerland; part of the big order he had won from us. I asked about them, and the repair department foreman said they were from an Army base in Fairbanks, Alaska, and had been air freighted down to have a broken head replaced! I asked why *both* had made the trip and was told that both the

All three bands on the liner S.S. United used Ludwig gear. Left to Right: Mickey Orner, Ralph Rodgers, Moe Rosenthal.

25" and 28" copper kettle timpani with trunks carried only one inventory number and therefore could never be separated. If the calf skin heads on all the rest of the three hundred and ninety-eight Slingerland timpani broke because of the aluminum flesh hoops being unwelded, Uncle Sam was in for a hell of a bill for the next fifty years, starting now! Compare the shipping costs of just the head and flesh hoop with shipping two timps and trunks round trip from Alaska. But of course they fly on Government planes.

Further inspection of that warehouse revealed many hundreds of the drums we had made during World War II. Were they being stored for World War III?? If this type of waste occurs in drums, imagine what the total waste must be for everything the Army buys every year! At the end of that day, I left the Quartermaster Depot for the last time, for shortly after that visit, they shifted their purchasing procedure and instead of buying directly from the manufacturer, they bought from retail dealers. The whole bid process everywhere (schools as well) consumes tremendous amounts of time. My heart always goes out to the unsung heros of bidding dealers who toil endlessly over bid invitations, both government and civilian, and never quite know at the end of the year whether they made any money for their business or not. Just one wrong price on a large bid can easily wipe out all the profit from a year's bidding. But that's all part of the making of a business– in this case the making of a drum company..... my drum company.

I once clipped a headline out of the *Music Trades* magazine published by Brian Majeski which read "Make A Profit– Everything Else Is Baloney". I placed it under the glass desk top and that slogan remained there in front of me for the next twenty years. It was very hard to live up to, as there are so many directions a chief operating officer is pulled and tugged by so many people both inside and outside of the organization.

The Roaring Beatle Era

After the introduction of The Beatles to America and their appearance on the Ed Sullivan Show, the drum world was inundated with a flood of teenagers who wanted to be drummers just like Ringo– and be famous and make a lot of money! The drum business in general took off. There is a saying, "A flood lifts all boats." I quote it here because all drum companies benefitted from the youngsters' desire to start up "garage bands". There were many bands set up in garages while parents' cars were parked outdoors! This was the era when drugs were becoming available to youngsters and parents found themselves in the unenviable position of having to cope with their children's temptations. A guitar to twang, a set of drums to beat up on.... anything they desired, they could have– just no drugs!

We had to crank up a night shift that started at 5:00 P.M. and ran until 1:00 A.M. six days a week. We were turning out a hundred sets per day with a crew of about 500 employees on two shifts. And at the same time we were buying up and digging up the neighorhood for expansion. Remember that we were expanding into a residential neighborhood. We started to receive complaints about the noise at night. The wood shop machines in particular were keeping them awake all hours of the night. I had to visit the neighbors up and down the block on Wabansia Avenue as well as Damen Avenue and invite them to plant tours followed by "jollification" at Boris's bar afterwards. We finally had to shut down certain machines like the stick lathes and scarfing machines at ten to quiet the neighborhood. My personal routine was also disrupted because I found it neccessary to frequently go home for dinner and return to the plant to tour the night shift. This was a vain attempt to shore up the quality that sank on that shift. Many times I found men sleeping in corners because they had worked a day shift somewhere else and had signed up for a night shift with me for the extra money. Half of the two hundred or so on the night shift were zombies! There were frequent fist fights in the alley behind the plant. It was a constant challenge, but we kept pretty close to our quota– 100 sets per day, mostly in oyster black pearl and all with the Ludwig logo on the front head of the bass drum. Our competition also gradually increased production and added oyster black pearl to their finish options. They could not, however, affix *Ludwig* to the front head!

Plant Theft

One rather ugly and costly incident worth mentioning occured in the midst of all the high-production commotion– it involved the theft of complete drum sets packed and ready for shipment. The day shift shipping department foreman reported these thefts. A frustrating thing about the thefts was that they broke up completed shipmentsof multiple outfit orders. I hired Pinkertons, the famous detective agency, who put a man in the shipping department posing as a Ludwig employee. For an entire summer the "spy" cozied up to all of the shipping room gang. He even met with some of them for breakfast at Halperin's Restaurant on the corner. After twelve weeks of daily surveillance he came up with nothing.

One day I was seated at my desk about 11:00 A.M. when I received a strange call from one of the drivers of a truck that had just picked up a load of drums. He said he had parked his truck just down the street and put up the hood so it would look like he was having engine trouble while he made this phone call. "I just picked up a shipment from your plant," he said, "and one of your employees named Jules propositioned me to buy a drum set for less than dealer cost. I don't believe in stealing from our customers. I appreciate my job and the business you give my company, so I'm tipping you off." I thanked him profusely and just sat there for some minutes, considering the situation. The thief he had "fingered" just happened to be one of my favorite employ-ees. As soon as I snapped out of my reverie, I called Pinkerton and they sent two men right out to pick up the culprit. We didn't really have any proof, so had to settle for a confession in exchange for immunity from prosecution. His confession detailed how he had been selling packed drum sets by just shoving them onto the tailgates of the wrong trucks and collecting down at the local tavern after his shift ended. I had Jules removed from the property and made it clear he should never return! To build a business requires constant vigilance against theft.

Another thievery episode occured just months later. The production manager reported a mysteriours disappearance of bongos from the night shift production. Having gotten nowhere with Pinkertons, I resolved to play detective myself. The first thing I did was to hire two off-duty Chicago cops to set up surveillance of the south wall at night. They were to pay special attention to the third floor, from which the bongos were disappearing. Their first night, I decided I would also have a look around. It was a dark night, but there was quite a bit of light from the city streetlights and the lights of the plant. I crouched in the bushes across the street. Suddenly a pair of hands clamped down on my shoulders. It was my own surveillance force. Those two cops had caught me!

My next plan was to creep up on the roof armed with stones to drop down on anyone tossing bongos to the street. All I got out of that effort was sore knees. The break came when we found long strings blackened with shoe polish hanging from the branches of some of the trees next to the building. I announced this over the public address system in the plant and demanded that the responsible parties step forward. They did, and I fired them. Before they left, I asked them what the string was for. They explained that they let the string down just above head level and placed a set of bongos on the window ledge attached to the string. Then, later at about 2:00 A.M., when the plant was closed, they returned and gave the string a stout tug and caught the bongos when they fell. It was so ingenious it was almost laughable.

In both cases, Julie with his outfit thefts and the night shift with its bongo thefts, the culprits explained that nobody from management seemed to have even noticed. Nothing had been said, so they kept it up. The lesson is Scream! Holler! Make a big noise! When you notice theft, let the culprits know you are closing in. They will stop these evil practices and you stem the losses as you continue to grow your business.

Japan Appears On The Horizon

The first sets made in Japan appeared in our country with the logo "Ludwig Star" on them. We protested this challenge to little or no avail. Finally I had to appeal to the U.S. Trade Commission for help and due to the efforts of our embassy in Tokyo the logo disappeared. The hurt, however, continued. We had new and dangerous competition from overseas. The defeated countries of the world looked to America as a fat new market and they would not be denied. Premier from England was making some headway here, as were Sonor and Trixon from Germany, Capelle from France, and Pearl and Yamaha from Japan.

Marshall Plan Benefits Foreign Companies

Our competitors abroad enjoyed great help from America at our expense. The first to benefit was Premier, who had been bombed out in the Battle of Britain air raids. The British government built a brand new state of the art one story plant in Leicester, 200 miles north of London. Then came government assistance for the Japanese drum companies, setting them up for renewed competition with Ludwig. It soon seemed to me that as soon as I met the threat of one competitor, a government was setting up two or three new ones for me to wrestle with! Still 1962 sales came in at $3,665,000 with a net of $225,000 (7.5%) after taxes. Our competitors wanted a part of it!

On the west coast the new drum shop was Professional Drum Shop, owned by Bob Yeager. Bob gave me my biggest order ever, which came as a surprise since it was given over the phone. He ordered 365 complete drums sets, to be shipped one per day. I was sitting on the fan tail (aft) of my second boat, a 35-foot cruiser, when I took the call in Chicago's Burnham Harbor and I celebrated with a cold beer. That was a lot of drums, and indicated Yeager's faith in the future!

Another young entrepreneur with faith in the future was (and still is) William F. Crowden. From humble beginnings as an orphan, he pulled himself up by his bootstraps to end up owning Franks Drum Shop! Franks Drum Shop is a story in itself. Frank Gault was one of three brothers who in the 1920s formed Dixie Music Company on Wabash Avenue in Chicago's downtown area know as the loop. Frank's brothers were musicians specializing in brass instrument performance. Dixie Music was destroyed by fire and George Gault was killed when he fell down the elevator shaft attempting to salvage sales records. With the dissolution of Dixie Music Co. in the mid 1930s, Frank Gault set up Chicago's second exclusive drum shop in 1937. (The first shop had been the one that my father and Theo established back in 1906.)

Naturally I made my presence known, jostling with my competitors for shelf and floor space. Although not a percussionist himself (he played trombone), Frank Gault had an easy low-key approach to serving his drum customers that quickly endeared him to the trade. Traveling drummers began to withhold their buying until they hit Chicago. The shop carried an enormous stock of accessories as well as the full range of all drum makes then available.

Although it was located on the fifth floor at 226 South Wabash Avenue, drummers quickly beat a path to his door, which was reached directly by the building elevator that opened directly to the inside of the shop! Throughout the years, even through the difficult years of the second World War, Frank Gault faithfully discharged his duties to the drumming fraternity. Finally age took its toll, and Frank Gault sold his shop to Maurie Lishon. Lishon was a popular and extremely talented longtime Chicago percussionist who was best known for his work at the radio (and later television) station WBBM. I had been supplying Maurie his drums for quite a few years and we got along well until he bought Frank's Drum Shop. (When he bought the shop, the name remained the same but the spelling changed; the apostrophe was dropped from Frank's: Franks Drum Shop.) It was my experience that Maurie's style of operation was to pressure his suppliers for delivery and discounts.

Crowden Applies For A Job

One day a very young Bill Crowden, who had been hanging around the shop helping out, was offered a steady job by Lishon. The offer included a 25% ownership position if Crowden stayed on for five years. Bill readily accepted. On the fifth anniversary, he reminded Maurie of the 25% ownership promise. Maurie told him to forget it because he had plans for his sons to come into the business. Bill quit immediately, and within months opened Drums Unlimited next door to Franks Drum Shop. Maurie called me down and expressed his displeasure in no uncertain terms. He gave me an ultimatum; do not sell to Bill Crowden or Franks would throw my drums out! I resented the ultimatum not only because it was an attempt to squeeze the upstart Drums Unlimited out of the drum business, but it was not in my opinion the proper way to conduct business. I refused, and Maurie did just what he said he would do. We lost a key account not just for Chicago, but at a regional (midwest) level. Franks Drum Shop was a $36,000.00 per year account which does not sound like much today, fifty years later, but it was certainly a lot in the 1960s.

That episode showed me a side of Maurie Lishon than many people never saw. While he was helpful and friendly to drummers, especially the young students, he was tough on his suppliers and exercised a vocabulary that matched his toughness.

Maurie took on the Rogers line and backed it furiously, as he was out to teach me a lesson. In the end it didn't really work; Crowden's volume steadily climbed through the years. I think Maurie even contributed to Bill's growth by regularly cussing him out which had the effect of sending prospects to him!

The reason I go into all of this is that it was an important lesson to me in Building A Drum Company. You cannot allow yourself to be threatened or intimidated. Gradually, little by little, the tide turned. Drums Unlimited gross sales eventually surpassed the sales of Franks Drum Shop. Maurie did not adapt to the changing situation gracefully; more vendors, customers, and even family members involved in the business began to experience his temper the way I had. Is any business really worth that? No, of course not.

Never throughout the years did I ever hear Bill Crowden express one unkind word toward Maurie Lishon. He regularly opened his shop on time early every morning whether he was sick or not and treated every customer in a quiet and dignified manner. It was not an easy life (anyone who thinks riding Chicago's elevated trains at 6:30 A.M. in the cold of a midwest winter sounds like fun should try it!) but it led to a steady sales increase.

Another drum shop owner who I feel "fought the good fight" was Bob Yeager, who as I mentioned earlier was the founder and proprietor of Hollywood's Professional Drum Shop. Bob was another congenial guy although he could express himself forcefully. One day a customer with a long overdue account came in to pay it up with $35.00 all in pennies. The customer threw the

Musical Director Paul Bouman directs the Grace Lutheran Church brass choir of River Forest, Illinois. The author is at the timpani.

pennies on the counter so violently that they spilled all over the floor. Bob came around the counter, grabbed him by the throat and showed him the door. A couple moments later the customer returned to meekly ask, "Does this mean I can't come to your Christmas party anymore?"

Timpani In Church Music
One day our church organist and music director, Paul Bauman, asked if I would play timpani on the high holy days along with the

Bill Crowden in his fabulous drum shop which became Chicago's drum headquarters in only ten years.

72

brass choir and adult choir. This was an interesting request that I didn't feel I could refuse. The timpani available was a pair of our early Ludwig & Ludwig tilting

marvelous million-dollar building through the years to view the manufacturing processes and drum collection. I had the opportunity to install a large wall cabinet display in my father's office specifically for pedals; it included some of the first drum pedals ever made along with his earliest pedals. This collection is now in my home, properly displayed in a lower-level museum.

In 1963, Joe Morello won the triple jazz crown as the best drummer in the nation by winning the jazz polls in *DownBeat, Playboy,* and *Music Maker* magazines.

We were able to burn the million-dollar mortgage two years later as sales and profits continued to climb. Sales for

Joe Morello always packed them in at his drum clinics. We did dozens of sold out clinics like this every year!

models, donated in 1933. This was fine with me because it meant I could tilt them and play from a seated position at all times. There is a lot of timpani and brass music available and I learned to play along with the choir using the regular hymnal as a guide. Pedal tuning allows quick pitch changes for different keys. After one rousing chorus where I really laid into the part, the pastor was so enthusiastic that he preceded his sermon with the words, "That's pounding it out for the Lord!" and struck the lectern a mighty blow for emphasis. I found timpani playing in church to be very rewarding and heartily recommend it!

Construction continued in 1963 on the massive corner building at 1736–1742 Damen Avenue. That addition included a new private executive suite with bathroom, state of the art electronics including a large television screen, air conditioning, and a sorely needed conference room. The conference room included shelves to accomodate the Wm. F. Ludwig private drum and pedal collection. This collection included the first drums and pedals of the company along with drums and pedals made by other companies as much as 100 years earlier. Thousands of drummers would pass through this

1966 Mortgage Burning: Sister Bettie participates in this joyous occasion!

1965 were $8,938,894 with a profit of $1,559,871 (taxes 51%), and 1966 saw sales of $12,348,415, profit of $1,854,281 (taxes 51%). The increase in 1966 was due to the outfit boom created by the rock and roll surge plus addition of a night shift.

Dick Schory and his Percussion Pops orchestra became a regular feature of our industry trade shows, playing in Chicago's Orchestra Hall (now known as Symphony Center). This helped mightily to draw attention to us and our sales reflected this. One year in Orchestra Hall, Dick had Joe Morello rise from the basement to the stage while playing his Ludwig silver sparkle outfit! It was a very effective setting to show off the talents of both Dick and Joe.

Ludwig Abroad

Ivor Arbiter really put Ludwig on the map in England as well as the continent. The perception grew that Ludwig drums were louder than the others. We thus opened the door for all our competitors to sell their makes abroad. Tastes were changing. Smaller groups were the "in" thing and big bands were passing from the scene. They were too expensive to maintain. Bass drum sizes were being reduced in the trade to as small as 20 ". A small rack tom was added to balance the bass drum and as drum sizes reduced, the cymbal sizes also declined. In spite of this, we featured larger outfits in the catalogs of the 1960s and the Supra Phonic 400 became the darling of the industry. The foundation for this acceptance was due to our use of a one-piece metal shell made of bronze which is a combination of brass and other exotic materials. Then followed the Acrolite model which became our best seller because the shell was of one-piece aluminum stock. The snare bed was widened. I am not at liberty to divulge what exactly the dimensions of the snare bed were; it is the secret of all Ludwig metal shell snare drums to this day. Competitors have striven mightily to uncover our secret but to no avail. Players swear our metal shell snare drums have response and clarity found in no other make.

The author and daughter Brooke with the Beatles and Dick Schory

1964 Sees Further Expansion Of The Head Plant

In answer to the ever growing demand for our *WeatherMaster* line of mylar heads, it was necessary to double the size of the head plant as well as connecting it to our main plant and the stand-alone building to the west, to provide undercover same-height floor space in areas that were all connected. Bud Slingerland was one day observed with binoculars peering through the upper windows at the rows of head presses so we covered all windows on the south side with plastic to preserve our privacy.

The Beatles Play Chicago

With the announcement that the Beatles would play one concert in Chicago, I wanted to express our gratitude to Ringo for all the exposure he had given us by choosing Ludwig and insisting that our name be displayed on the front bass drum head. My mind went back to the glorious gold-plated drums of the glory days of Ludwig & Ludwig and the wonderful imitation gold plating on the black beauty models of the mid 1920s. A special gold-plated snare drum was made which I presented to Ringo in thanks for all his illustrious name had done in building our company in the early 1960s. The presentation meeting was arranged by Dick Schory (at far right in photo on the previous page). Ringo seemed grateful to receive it but for a long time I was disconcerted by the image of the last time I saw the drum–under the arm of a Chicago cop. Years later Ringo was able to assure me that he had it safely stored in one of his homes in his native England and still played it occasionally.

Wm. F. Ludwig Sr. and Dick Richardson discussing production of Musser instruments at the LaGrange Musser facility.

Because of all the activity abroad, I made frequent trips overseas with our wonderful export manager Frank Baxpehler who was a master of six languages and able to forge very special bonds with the distributors he appointed in the countries of the world. It was important to visit each country to study the people, and of course you had to appoint one, and only one, distributor in each to set the prices in the currency of that particular country. It was all very glamorous and exciting. Frank Baxpehler proved to be the greatest export manager in the music business and grew our volume abroad to over $4,000,000 annually!

The Frank Arsenault Story

I had had some correspondence with Frank Arsenault, who was New England's champion snare drummer. He arrived totally unannounced one day in December, saying flat out, "I quit my job with Pitney-Bowes and have all my personal possessions in the car outside and I have come to work for you!" It was a real shock! Worse,

Frank Arsenault and the author at a Tacoma, Washington, drum clinic.

it was 4:00 P.M. and he had no place to stay! I put him up at the local YMCA and told him to report to my office in the morning. He did and I put him on the assembly bench until I could figure out how to use him. My father came across him and wanted to know what he was doing there. I explained that it was just temporary. Every day thereafter he hounded me to fire Frank! The next week I got him placed in three drum corps as instructor at $10.00 per night. This, plus his half-day at Ludwig, saved Frank and he went on to become our full time clinician on the road 50 weeks of the year. He was also especially helpful in setting up and dismantling our large displays. We were now displaying at twelve conventions per year, both educational and dealer shows. Frank Arsenault would set up the display and man it each day, answering all manner of rudimental drumming questions. He became a pillar of strength backing up our sales force and he contributed mightily to our growth over the next seven years.

Ludwig Purchases Musser Marimba Company

In 1965 the educators held their national convention in Kansas City and I pulled out all the stops. Our massive pre-fab display stretched for seventy-five feet and we rented the famed Pendergast Suite on the top floor of the Muellback Hotel. Pendergast was the politician who "discovered" Harry Truman and elevated him to Senator first and eventually the Presidency near the close of the War in 1945. We threw a party for all of the exhibitors and most of the 175 exhibitors attended. (Educators were not invited, for the Music Educators Conference felt that it was too late to keep them up.)

It went very late, to 3:00 A.M. and everyone had a huge time. The next day while relaxing in my suite which was separate from the Pendergast Suite because I was President of the Music Industry Council, I was approached by Dick Richardson. Dick was owner and CEO of the Musser Company, which he offered to sell to me in recognition of the fabulous sales job we were accomplishing as a distributor of Musser products. Dick said, "I am struggling to keep up with your orders and I don't want to incur additional debt to expand my plant in LaGrange (Illinois, a Chicago suburb), so how about I sell out to you?" My response was, "I accept your offer, and for book," book meaning the value of the business at that point in time. We shook hands and it was a done deal. That's the way gentlemen of good faith do business. Then the lawyers got into it for the next three months, but as far as Dick and I were concerned, Ludwig owned Musser. We immediately set about enlarging the Musser plant and investing in the smaller Kitching Company which came along with the deal. Kitching made elementary mallet instruments which were sold directly to schools, bypassing dealers. When I tried to distribute the Kitching line through our regular dealer channels, I failed miserably and phased the entire division out two years later. But owning the Musser company put us truly in the limelight around the world as the company with Total Percussion. We became "Ludwig– Total Percussion" and we still hold that title and claim to this day since no one else makes all the percussion items in our line in this country. Sure, there are distribution setups of products made abroad, but I mean *made in this country*. That is Ludwig– Total Percussion!

Improving on Beethoven

About this time (the mid 1960s), I learned that my Dad's sister had never been to a symphony concert and I resolved to redress this situation. I picked a rousing concert with a lot of timpani passages: Ludwig Van Beethoven's Third Symphony,the "Eroica". I made sure our seats were in the first row center in the first balcony and my dear aunt seemed to enjoy the spectacle of one of the world's great symphonic ensembles sounding their very best for forty five minutes. The timpanist was Donald Koss who studied with my former teacher, Ed Metzenger. Don Koss is among the world's greatest timpanists and has held his position with the Chicago Symphony Orchestra longer than any of his predecessors– 34 years and counting! Towards the end of the symphony, I leaned over to my aunt's ear and whispered, "Watch the timpanist. He's going to play a gigantic solo."

Soon after the concert ended and as the audience thundered its hearty approval, my dear aunt asked, "How did you know he was going to do that?" I was stunned. My aunt thought that the timpanist just made up his part as he went along and that he was talented enough to just make himself fit in. That got me thinking. How many other members of the public are unaware that timpanists and percussionists in general actually have written parts to play? And what really surprises them is when you tell people that the gong player has notes to play as well! The lesson here is that we can never stop explaining to all the public and as early as possible all about music and the instruments in the orchestra. Don't ever take the public's knowledge for granted!

Case in point. Early in my sister's marriage, I decided to expose my brother-in-law to a symphony concert. When it finished, the conductor took many bows and my brother-in-law said, "I don't see why he is taking all that credit– he didn't do a thing all evening!" He felt that since the conductor hadn't played any instrument, thay should get rid of him. To reciprocate, Jim took me hunting one week and it was without doubt the worst week of my life. I hated to kill living birds and the worst was preparing them for the freezer! Touche'.

A Million Dollar Stumble

In 1958 my father made a trip to his birth place at Nenderoth, Germany. He found it about the same as when he had left seventy-three years earlier. Only four more houses had been built! He attended the Frankfurt Messe or Music Fair and there he met Michael M. Paiste, the patriarch of the famous Paiste cymbal manufacturing family. He was quite a remarkable fellow, having started in 1906 pounding out brass disks in St. Petersburg, Russia, where he learned the basics of cymbal manufacturing. When the Russian Revolution happened in October of 1917, he slipped over the border into Estonia with his entire family and business belongings, and set up shop in that country. From there, in 1939, he again fled westward, into Gdynia, Germany, where he started up again. He moved again in 1945 to Schleswig-Holstein, Germany. Sons Robert and Toomas moved the firm to Switzerland to avoid the disruptions associated with wartime Germany. In 1951 the Paiste gong shop was set up in Rendsburg and in 1957 a second plant was erected in Nottwil-LU/Switzerland which is Paiste's home today.

My father purchased some samples from M.M. Paiste and brought them back with him. I found them too thick for the American taste but the price for the bottom of the line was extremely attractive and we ordered a few of them. These cymbals were stamped with our name, creating an exclusivity which we used to sell outfits. We ordered 20,000 cymbals per year for several years and received nothing but good comments about them. So far, so good, as they say.

During one of my visits to London, Ivor Arbiter suggested that I try the first-line Paiste cymbals. I did, and still felt that they were too thick. We ordered 75, mostly to show at the Chicago convention that summer. My father warned that Avedis Zildjian, patriarch of the Zildjian family, would cut me off. I reminded him that we were their largest account and went ahead confidently

with the display. When Avedis came to our room (we displayed in hotels in those days– this was 1964), he flew into a towering rage and cut me off just like Dad said he would. This was a serious blow but the Paiste brothers, Robert and Toomas, assured me they would stand by me. We worked out a contract giving us exclusivity for all of North America and Mexico. In return we ordered 2,000 units per month. With this order, they returned to Switzerland and showed the order commitments to their bankers to help them secure credit to finance factory expansion and modernization. Still the product was believed too thick and heavy for the American market. I went over to Paiste's with Bob Yeager of

Robert and Toomas Paiste (above left) show members of the Ludwig sales staff the cymbal making steps at their plant near Lucerne, Switzerland.

the Professional Drum Shop in Hollywood to thin the whole line out. We stayed there a week and reset the standards of thickness throughout the line.

One day our returned goods department reported a cymbal returned broken. This was not particularly unusual to me since cymbals are beaten up pretty severely and sometimes cracks occur. When I saw this particular cymbal, however, my heart filled with dread. There was a huge chunk out of it as if an animal with a very powerful bite had chewed into it like a sandwich! The next day another cymbal came back with a bite out of it. And the next. And so on. I reported the situation right away to the Paiste brothers and they came right over from Switzerland. By the time they arrived, the returns were lying in a tidy pile. The Paiste brothers looked them over and stated that the players were striking them too hard. I took them to a show in town and one of their cymbals broke right in front of them. They maintained that the drummer was hitting them too hard. The drummer responded. "If I don't hit them this hard I'll lose my job!"

Now we had a standoff. Ludwig vs. Paiste. By this time we were accumulating so many returns that we had to set aside a special vault in our new basement just for the thousands and thousands of broken cymbals! We were replacing each and every broken cymbal from inventory, and expected Paiste to make good in return. When push came to shove, however, they refused to replace any of the 4,000 broken cymbals.

Now it was time to bring in our attorney. He worked out a compromise in which they would give us a special deduction of 10% on all future purchases. The ink was barely dry on this contract when they raised their prices 10%! I was skewered! I was on the horns of an awful dilemma– every day cymbals were being returned and every day we replaced them; some as many as four times.

Sometimes you have to face the agony of defeat and admit it. We stopped sending any further orders and canceled all that we had on order. We ceased filling orders and gave away the entire remaining stock–thousands of cymbals. I never totalled up the frightful cost of this misadventure but we had to have lost at least a million dollars. Not once did my father tell me, "I told you so!" What a guy!

Another Ludwig On The Horizon

Through these years my son William had been growing up experiencing a normal education laced with a little drumming. From his earliest years he saw and heard my father and I playing duets together on the national holidays. That stimulated his interest in percussion at an early age. I didn't sit him down at a pad like my father had done with me, for I felt he would have enough inspiration around to learn percussion on his own. And he did. When the Beatle boom hit he had to have a Ringo-style outfit and a band, which was called *The Cheasepeake Leopard Affair*. In no time my once serene househould was turned into a rock and roll studio! I soon learned the agony of transporting his equipment on any travel date in the neighborhood.

Bill III was with me at many international conventions and met and made many friends in our country as well as overseas. We are so proud of him!

Wm. F. Ludwig III began his international travel at a tender age; here he overlooks London's Hyde Park at age 9.

What Goes Up Must Come Down

Finally in the summer of 1967 we moved in to our big 40,000 square-foot addition just in time for the big bust. That's right, you heard it– the big bust. It happened so insidiously; first a single dealer cancellation. Then another. We were still programmed to produce 100 4-piece sets per day. We didn't know how to handle overproduction. Orders for drum sets just stopped, and we were only half-way through the massive 365 set order from Bob Yeager! There was a shift in interest from the Beatles style to Bebop and cooler music. In just three weeks our order backlog sank and we began to make plans to discontinue the night shift. Three more weeks and we did. So, what goes up *always* comes down– and every boom usually has a bust right behind. We scrambled, and I mean really scrambled. As all of the order backlog withered, dealers started calling to ask permission to return their unsold stock of drum sets! Producing 100 sets per day quickly used up our storage space, including the space in the brand new building. I got on the phone to leading school dealers to restore the school business. So did my competitors. Within a week we had finally stemmed the production tide, but what to do with the hundreds of drum sets boxed with nowhere to go? We held some mighty fire sales!

Layoffs followed with the union protesting every inch of the way. We cranked up our advertising in the school papers as well as designing new school merchandise brochures. As a cost-cutting measure, we indefinitely suspended the twice-yearly *Ludwig Drummer* magazines. It was really chaotic and as the famous British war time leader Winston Churchill said, "These are the times that try men's souls."

Fiberwood Drum Sticks

I received a call from Bob Yeager to meet him at O'Hare airport. In a coffee shop, he very secretively unwrapped a pair of drumsticks that looked and felt like hickory but were straight as a die. Bob explained that they were appearing on the West Coast and were made by Bob Brilhart, President of Fiberwood Corporation and that they might replace hickory drumsticks. My heart leapt for joy! To be free of the vagrancies of wood with the warping problems, splitting, breaking, etc. would indeed be heaven. I went for the Fiberwood hook line, and sinker. I signed an exclusive contract with Brilhart for 100,000 pairs of sticks without proper testing.

At the distribution agreement signing; (L-R): Robert Brilhart, Wm. F. Ludwig Jr., F.K. Peppler

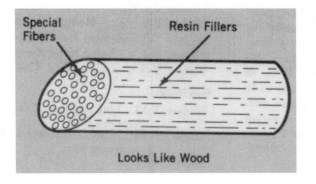

I played hard with them; rimshots by the hundreds with no breakage. And they were uniformly straight and would never warp. I could visualize the dawn of a new era in percussion. Trouble-free sticks, and beaters, too!

We got out the literature toute de suite and when the first shipments came in they went right out into the eager hands of a waiting public. In about three months a pair was received back in our return goods department. They were badly "chewed" right on the shoulder where most rim shots are positioned. Soon others came back and again we had to replace them. Finally, with thousands coming back I had to call a halt on ordering further stock and started the devastating procedure of eating crow! Bob Brilhart said there was no way he could fix the stick. Apparently the same fibers used to make waterproof reeds for wind instruments would not qualify for being smacked repeatedly on a drum hoop. It was a dud and cost us dearly. It cost me not only dollars, but also shook my confidence. I felt that my father was now giving me the "eye" and there were question marks in it. I had failed to test the product thoroughly. Hickory wood dowels were saved to continue throughout eternity to be the raw material of choice for drumstick manufacturers.

Musser marimbas and vibes were still being manufactured and sold, as were our wonderful five models of timpani. Gradually the school business picked up as well and of course one can't leave out the marching drum market which we had dominated for so long– both the American Legion and Veterans of Foreign Wars drum and bugle corps.I mention these heartaches because they are all part of business. You think of something different or someone brings you something new and you don't want your competitor to hear about it. So, instead of testing it thoroughly, you push it into production and let the trade do your testing for you. This method of testing can be very costly! Still, sometimes this is the best way with drums because we at the factory just want it to succeed so badly we rush it into market and get banged on the head if things don't work out.

In the mid 1960s we found that publishing a new catalog every year was just too tiring and expensive so we moved to a format called "just in time". That meant that when we started to run low on catalogs we began work on the replacement, hoping to get it published just as we ran out of the old catalog. This didn't always work, however, and there were many years when we were entirely out of catalogs and relied on hastily assembled flyers and brochures to fill the breach. The 1967 catalog showed the completed building on Damen Avenue. A solid block of buildings all joined and with level floors from St Paul Avenue to Willow Street. That was a distance of 212 feet, with three floors and a full basement; 85,000 square feet in all!

The 1967 catalog showed an ever wider choice of finishes including twelve pearl finishes which could be laid up in the shop in any variety the customer requested. There were lacquer finishes in multi-color configurations (blue and silver were the most popular), a mahogany finish for the classical percussionists, and we had a new high-tension stainless steel line of marching drums. The catalog was 104 pages plus a four page front and back high-gloss cover. It cost a fortune!

Pay Up, Mr. Ludwig, or Crash!

Even though sales were up ($13,300,000), as were profits ($932,500), we had added monumental overhead. Property taxes and mortgage payments totaled $3,500,000, so all was not as rosy as one might think as the 1960s drew to a close. Bud Slingerland had moved into a handsome and efficient one-story factory which he paid for out of his stock market profits made on Zenith radio stock. It was located just up the road from us in Niles, Illinois, which lowered his taxes. (Not just property taxes! The City of Chicago had a head tax of $5.00 per employee per month which adds up over a year!)

The foreign competition continued to build up also: Premier, Pearl, Tama, Yahama, and Sonor.

So I had to come up with a heavy repayment for my dozen additions over the years to this date– 1967. This was a burden I hadn't counted on since business had

20,000 hickory drum stick dowels stacked on receiving skids and handled with fork lifts; ready for transfer to the stick department

always been up year after year. But as my father always preached– avoid expansion because you never know what's down the road. On the other hand we were seiz-

ing the whole market and the lure of expansion was irresistable. But my father had been through that and knew full well what might lie ahead. That's youth, of course, always pushing ahead while the elderly who have experienced bad times urge caution.

The Beatles Invade My House

My son's booming career with his band resulted in endless rehearsing in our basement. Before the Beatles boom we had other beetles in the house– the crawling kind. Come to think of it, the crawling beetles disappeared when the musical Beatles arrived. Bill was really getting interested in drumming; he became section leader in the Downers Grove High School Band and really looked manly charging down Main Street sparking the whole 12-man percussion section in attacking every Sousa march! I was busting my buttons! His bubbling personality always countered my increasing gloominess as business problems mounted and foreign competition revved up. It was so great watching him progress year by year from boyhood to manhood as he participated in percussion along the way. I arranged for private lessons for Bill, not trusting my temperament as an amateur teacher. I hired the late Herman Wiegman to come to our house once a week and fixed up a little studio in our basement. Herman was a leading percussionist and professional teacher with a sparkling personality who possessed the very latest drum instruction technique designed to excite and encourage his many students.

In a few years Bill was ready for more advanced training so I switched him to the very eminent late, Bobby Christian, who taught in his Oak Park home. His teaching studio was the second floor of a coach house behind his house, which was full of drums. Bobby was the foremost percussion personaility in Chicago and a regular on television and radio shows. In addition, Bobby was the concert master in Dick Schory's Percussion Pops Orchestra which was making hit recordings on the RCA label. These albums were doing much to fan the ever-growing flames of popular percussion listening and we all owe a tremendous debt of gratitude to Dick Schory and Bobby Christian for their sensational recordings.

My son never wanted for professional guidance and inspiration, not to mention the stacking of the old rope drums on our patio and drumming with Dad and Grandad on the high holidays such as Memorial Day and Independence Day.

A Rising Conflict Over Hand Grips

Through all these years we had continued publishing the quarterly bulletins of the National Association For Rudimental Drummers, N.A.R.D. In 1967 we were up to Bulletin No. 118. My father started these bulletins in 1933 with the founding of the N.A.R.D. during the American Legion Convention of 1933 in Chicago. Ludwig & Ludwig had a big marching drum display in the centrally located Lyon & Healy five-story corner store (now a McDonalds) at Jackson Blvd. and Wabash Avenue. On the second day of that convention, a photograph was made of the thirteen very prominent drummers gathered at this display. These men came to be known as the founders of the National Association of Rudimental Drummers with my father as secretary. As secretary, he became the author of the quarterly bulletins.

Front row, left to right: **Harry Thompson, George A. Robertson, Bill Flowers, Bill Kieffer, Bill Hammond, Joe Hathaway, Larry Stone, Roy Knapp**
Back Row, left to right: **Wm. F Ludwig, Heinie Gerlach, J. Burns Moore, Billy Miller, Ed Straight**

The purpose of the organization was to protect and preserve a system of standardized rudiments as an anchor for all marching and concert classical drumming.

My father laid out twenty-six of the old rudiments of drumming from the Civil War instruction book written in 1861 by George B. Bruce. This book, "Bruce And Emmett Drum And Fife Instructor," was the same book my father received his lessons from in 1890 from drummer John Catlin of the Illinois National Guard.

The idea of choosing twenty-six rudiments from a large compliment of rudiments was to focus the student's attention on those rudiments appearing in most marches and concert pieces. It was no coincidence that there were twenty-six letters in the English alphabet. You learn the letters of the alphabet, then string letters together and form words. You learn the rudiments and string them together to form rhythms. It is as simple as that, but I feel it is remarkable that my father thought of it in this wonderful manner, especially when you consider he never passed beyond the eighth grade in his schooling.

During all the years of my father's life, he never failed to write up a quarterly bulletin, have it mimeographed, and mailed out on time!

I feel that the greatest feature of the N.A.R.D. was that membership was awarded only to those who took the entrance examination from a member in good standing. My father, together with others such as the great rudimentalist J. Burns Moore of New Haven, CT., had chosen thirteen rudiments from the complete list of twenty six rudiments as the most "essential" rudiments and these became the membership test rudiments. These were to be played open–closed–open to teach complete control at all speeds. Open means very slow, closed means very fast; mastery of the rudiments can be demonstrated by playing both in one continuous cycle. Many applicants failed this test and were admonished to practice and apply for retesting. That was the idea; to get young people practicing the rudiments! And it worked! Accompanying the application, a fee of .25 was required. In return we sent out a membership card which was renewable each year. This resulted in ever larger accounting and secretarial chores, which by 1967 amounted to hundreds of hours of time and considerable expense which the company simply wrote off.

We printed thousands and thousands of N.A.R.D. rudimental sheets and applications. Many band directors wrote, "Bill, thank God for the N.A.R.D. rudimental sheets you put out every year. I am not a percussionist so each fall when the new season starts, I just hand out these free rudiment sheets to my drummers and say 'Here– practice these and learn them if you want to play in the band!' "

Through the years band directors began to look to Ludwig as a company that was interested in their problems– not just one whose only interest was in selling percussion equipment and making money. This was a very subtle way of doing business. The competition never caught on! Score one for our side!

Slowly, ever so gradually, the great universities of our land began to create music departments starting, of course, with the piano. The piano is a complete musical instrument with a long and deep heritage leading back to the forerunner, the harpsichord. The harpsichord has a similar action to the piano but with only two strings per note in place of today's three strings and the total range was only six octaves instead of the piano's eight-octave range. Next, music departments added stringed instrument studies; violin, cello, double bass. These were followed by the rest of the instrumental family including brass, woodwinds, and finally percussion. (The heads of these departments were, of course, imminent players of virtuoso levels.)

Classical drumming differs from marching percussion, but until recently the hand grips were the same. Around 1960, some leaders in the percussion teaching field began to question the use of the "traditional" marching grip when applied to concert performance. The traditional grip is necessary when carrying a field drum on a sling. Due to the angle of the drum as it hangs, the left hand must be positioned to bring the stick over the counterhoop. With the advent of the over-the-shoulder "vest" carrier which we introduced at about this time, it was possible to easily strike the head while holding both sticks in a matched grip. This launched a controversy which may well rage for centuries! Matched grip versus traditional grip. My father, as titular head of the traditional grip fraternity, stoutly attacked the matched grip group which was led by some of the most important key customers such as Paul Price and Jack McKenzie at the University of Illinois, my old Alma Mater. Slowly, like the sands in an hourglass, the conflict escalated. My father began to, at first, condemn the match grip privately, then openly. This put me squarely in the middle, for I could see the advantages of teaching and using the matched grip in ALL percussion performance.

I began to question my father's logic in attacking our customers over how to hold the sticks. Once while visiting the National Music Camp at Interlochen, Michigan, I sat on a dock on the lake with Jack McKenzie, the percussion master at both the summer camp and the University of Illinois in the wintertime. We were watching his children (he had five) play in the gentle lake water when suddenly Jack said, "Can you get your father to stop writing Joe Maddy (president and founder of the camp) letters condemning my teaching and trying to get me fired?" I must have been sitting there with my mouth hanging open. Here was a national figure in the percussion world in charge of suggesting makes and models of percussion equipment to be purchased by two large organizations, and he was under attack by the Ludwig Drum Company, represented by my father. Talk about foolhardy!

I literally could not wait to get back to the office. When I did, I confronted my Dad over the grip issue. He stoutly stood his ground that the traditional grip was the ONLY grip allowed in drumming and I on the other hand pleaded for reason. These were our customers!

On the one hand, we were ad-

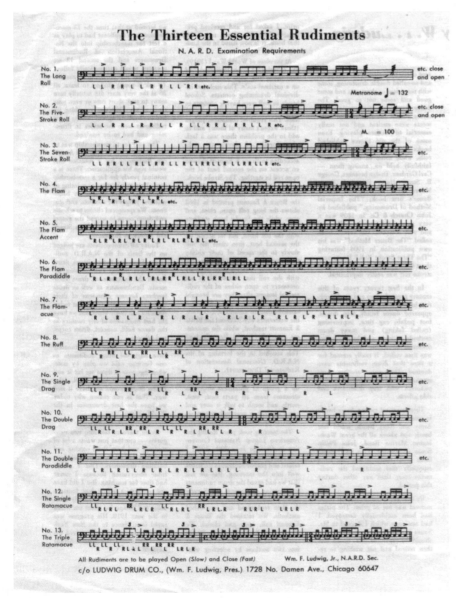

vertising and "clinicing" our heads off, beseaching people to buy our products; and on the other hand, the head of the corporation was maligning them! And it got worse. Whenever visitors arrived to tour the plant which was now large enough for high school band tours, I had them come through our big new board room to see my father's private collection of drums and pedals from the old days. I had to monitor the introductions carefully because my Dad couldn't resist ending his remarks with a tirade against the matched grip and those who advocated it. At that point I would interrupt and start the group filing out of the room behind the tour guide. I also had to monitor his correspondence by insisting that his secretary read from her shorthand notes every letter he dictated. These were often riddled with slurs against the "match grippers" and "college professors" and I would alter these sections or remove them completely. He never caught on! Call it revolt, call it deceitful, call it what you will; but I wasn't about to permit my father, at the age of eighty-nine years, to throw out all the good will and customer confidence over a stupid issue like the proper stick grip. For the remaining years of his life, I stood between my father and disaster while the matched grip slowly took over the drum world.

These were the unhappy final years of his life. He died in 1973 at the good old age of 94 and I did my best to care for him and make him as comfortable as I could. His last day on earth he pulled me over and whispered, "Thanks for taking care of the business and thanks for having such a nice family." With these final words ringing in my ears, I left him for the last time, satisfied that I had done my part in bringing him happiness.

For six months after his passing, I left his office and desk calendar as he had left it on July 7th, 1973. After this period of respectful reverance, I moved into his office and assumed the visual appearance of chief operating officer of the company; a role I had actually assumed a full year previously. I ordered new furniture and drapes and installed a large-screen television set. Frank Baxpehler, my confidante and export manager, installed a ninety-gallon aquarium with internal lights to add some color to the office, and I settled in.

Founder and father Wm. F. Ludwig Sr. (at age 90) demonstrates the traditional grip on our patio.

Memorial to my father erected in my home in 1975

A Three-Legged Defense Is Born

The world news was full of America's three-legged military defense: land-based intercontinental missiles buried deep in silos across the western plains, intercontinental bombers at the ready in Omaha, and finally the wonderful deeply submerged Trident submarines, each with 32 missiles ready to go against any assailant at a moment's notice. Talk about planning! I thought it was wonderful protection during the cold war. So I thought, "We also need a three-tiered defense in the drum world to protect us not only from domestic competitors, but also from overseas manufacturers."

The first level of our defense would be our already solid and world-reknowned wood-shell line. The second line of defense would be our new stainless-steel line, and the third leg of defense would be the marvelous *Vistalite* plexiglass line. Expecially formidable was the multi-colored Vistalite line. Both the stainless steel and vistalite lines were exclusive to Ludwig. Since manufacturing two complete additional lines of shells would require additional space, I kept buying up the neighborhood– a total of twenty-seven houses in all. A total of an acre of land would be needed for a truly giant four-story addition with *no basement*. I had about had it with floor load problems and needed a ground floor for raw material storage of really heavy tonnage. A receiving department was laid out with hydraulic leveling lifts to allow a fork truck to drive into a truck to pull out a load of lumber, drum stick dowels, coiled steel for hoops, and tons and tons of tubing for stands of all types.

The second floor was devoted to the metal polishing department, IBM mainframe bookkeeping machines, engineering, drafting files, tables, and a convenient tool room for the development of new products as well as machinery and dies to make them. The third floor would be set aside for all assembly and everything required to make the entire Vistalite line, and later the Tivoli line of lighted drums.

A Hunt For $2,000,000

To support this "Triad" defense would require some fancy financial footwork so with the aid of our longtime certified public accountant, Mr. John Seybold, we located the Prudential Insurance Company's capital investment officer, Mr. Donald Heitzler. When Mr. Heitzler arrived in my office, I couldn't believe someone so young could be in charge of so much loan money! He didn't bat an eye when after a quick tour of the plant, I asked for one

million dollars. (And later a rollover to a second million when it became obvious that we would be woefully short.) So in the summer of 1969, construction began on the 62,500 square-foot building with plenty of parking spaces. (The City of Chicago would not issue a permit to build without parking spaces provided; one space for every four employees.) This marvelous new facility was constructed of concrete with columns extending down to clay pan ninety-five feet into the earth. That depth was so fewer columns would be required. There was a 250 lb. per square foot floor load limit up to and including the fourth floor.

Two elevators were included, bringing us up to a total of nine elevators in the entire Damen Avenue complex. This made us a very valuable maintenence customer to the faithful Ewart Elevator Company! The contractor followed the architects' design of "post-tensioned" construction– a relatively new type of construction designed to allow maximum floor load with widely separated columns. This entailed laying cable running one way only and mounted on four-inch posts, all to be surrounded with freshly poured concrete. Then as it dried, the tension was increased weekly with the use of powerful tensioning machines along the West wall. It was all very exciting to watch and seemed to move well along with completion in the following year, 1970.

Celebrating the completion of the final factory building on Damen Avenue

Bud Bows Out

Meanwhile, up Milwaukee Avenue, Bud Slingerland elected to sell his company to a book publisher– McMillan and Co. Publishing, a really large one-billion dollar company publicly traded on Wall Street. The story I heard was that someone on the board of directors got the idea that since McMillan sold tons of textbooks to schools they should buy up other companies that sold goods to schools. (That is called "Horizontal" integration.) So they bought Oswald Uniform Company (the largest uniform company in the world), C.G. Conn (the world's largest band instrument company, in Elkhart, Indiana) and then the Slingerland Drum Company in Niles, Illinois, just up the street from us. That plan was just plain goofy; the type of plan that spawns disaster.

Bud wanted out and I like to think that I had something to do with it! The 33-year-old plan to concentrate in the school field was panning out. I am sure that with all our frenetic activity and many lines of shells, he must have grown weary of trying to keep up.

The Triad Drum Defense

In 1971 we moved into our latest addition of 62,500 square feet– three times the space of our original building on Damen and St Paul Avenue in 1937. As usual I had not allowed for capital to design and build the machinery required to construct the stainless steel and plexiglass lines, so had to borrow more on a short-term basis. These dies and cutting machines were very special. The stainless steel shells, for instance, could not be drilled with our regular wood drilling equipment because the steel was too hard. The holes to permit mounting of lugs and holders had to be punched into the shells. This required heavy-duty punch presses and a full complement of various spaced dies. Similarly, drilling plexiglass for the Vistalite line presented a great many problems. The speed and pressure of all multi-mounted drill heads cracked the material. With help from our own engineering department and the outside, we learned to position the drill heads to enter the material one drill at a time rather than all four contacting the surface simultaneously.

We found it was impossible to saw plexiglass without moving the work evenly across the face of the saw. Especially at the end of a cut, the piece would shift just enough to "jiggle", spoiling the lap when it was heated and bent into the drum shell shape. The answer to this one was to clamp the piece solidly in place using air pressure and moving a circular saw down the length of the cut, eliminating the jiggle. We found that by placing the saw at an angle, we could obtain a slant-edge which would permit us to place another piece of a contrasting color and provide a "V" vessel to put the epoxy resin

into. After a few hours of hardening, we had multicolored shell material.

Heating And Bending A Multi-Colored Shell

The next question was: Could a multi-colored panel of plexiglass be heated and molded around a circular form without melting the epoxy resin? This was a very dramatic moment. No one knew the answer to that one, so we tried it. The day of that test will forever live in my memory. All engineers and sales people were called to the Vistalite section in the new building and we watched literally breathlessly as a panel of multicolored Vistalite was heated up, then removed from the heating oven and wrapped around a mold. It did not fall apart! We cheered and I felt something like scientific researchers must feel when their team makes a great breakthrough. I was so excited and happy that I called Bill Crowden at Drums Unlimited and told him about our great success and made him promise to come out to my house after dinner to see this marvelous new development. I honestly believed we were making drum history.

Bill came out in the evening and I had a dozen sample squares placed strategically around my living room. I was shaking with excitement. Each sample looked more attractive than the next. Bill Crowden surveyed them coolly and calculatingly, without expressing nearly the excitement I tried to convey. He must have thought me an idiot!

With the success of the multi-colored Vistalite assured, Frank Baxpehler put his advertising department to work and produced some really brilliant and unique brochures and catalogs. The theme he originated was "Stripe Up The Band". Next the production department began a campaign of dazzling me with as many "far-out" striped and multi-colored designs as they could dream up. I was in heaven! Each day when I entered that department on my morning plant-wide inspection, they came up with another pattern. It was "colored pattern Vistalite Du Jour"– the color pattern of the day! It was all so colorful and beautiful I used to stand in the middle of that 10,000 square foot department and allow my eyes to feast on all the colors. We were indeed a colorful company!

One Leg of The Triad Gets Wounded

Amongst all this joy, returned goods again punctured my balloon. It was only a pin prick at first, but having been through this before I knew that this snafu would escalate as most of the others had through the years– cymbals, fiberwood drum sticks, plastic tension knobs and lugs on the Standard Line. This time it was a shell returned with the pearl finish shifting due to shrinkage!

I have already recited how through the years various chemical companies had found the production of pyralin for drum shells to be unprofitable. First the DuPont Chemical Company, then Monsanto Chemical Company, and now World Wide Chemical Company based in Italy. World Wide owned all of the molds and production facilities globally and therefore had an exclusive market. We, and I mean all percussion companies, were entirely at their mercy. They had done something different to the backing of the pyralin sheets, causing them to shrink weeks after being affixed to the drum shells. The flood of returned drums rose and eventually we had to set aside an entire floor to accomodate thousands and thousands of returned drums. As the philosopher once said– if it isn't one thing, it's another! What to do?

We replaced many of the shells but then the replacements also began to shrink. It couldn't go on this way, so we had to temporarily discontinue the entire pearl-covered drum line. That hurt us where we lived since we had been covering wood shells with marine and black pearl and sparkle pyralin since 1928!

Salvation– Of Sorts

One night I was sitting in my recreation room at home gazing at the fabulous Ludwig collection of antique drums when my eye caught sight of a particularly appealing tacked head design on an Eli Brown drum made in 1841. I knew, of course, that the reason for the tacking on the old dogs of war was to fasten the lap securely since glue was slow drying in earlier times. Then it hit me; here we were all those years later suffering from a similar ailment. Why not apply a band-aid to the patient until a cure can be found half way around the world? I literally could not wait to get to the plant the next day, and arrived shortly before 5:00 A.M. I excitedly called a meeting of my entire staff; sales, production, and especially engineers, for 8:00 A.M.. Some of the twenty or so stumbled in still carrying their morning coffee. I quickly launched into a brief history of tacking of the very old rope drums and brought this up to date as a cure to halt the shrinking of the pyralin sheets.

One advantage of my plan was that it would be a semi-exclusive one since all the other drum companies using World Wide as a source for pyralin would suffer the same problem. If I could fix it before my competitors, I could have some easy sailing.

Alas! Once again I was the only one in the room who approved of tacking shells as a solution.

Engineering To The Rescue

Once again engineering ability came to our rescue. At that emergency meeting (similar to ER; the emergency room in a hospital!) our Chief Engineer finally spoke up, suggesting rivets in place of tacks. He explained that tiny rivets could be imbedded into the overlap to steady the pearl covering and prevent gapping at the critical lap section of the shell. At that juncture, John Mahoney, who I had hired as controller in July of 1968, spoke up with the caveat that the shrinking might pull on the rivets much the way a person's shirt pulls on the buttons when a shirt is too small. (Which is exactly what happened.)

In the heat of the emergency and faced with growing losses, I ordered that the engineering department set up a riveting department as an extra and final process of drum shell manufacture.

Gang drills held in fixtures in neat rows and evenly spaced entered the shell just deep enough to allow the rivets to drop into the holes and rest flush with the material. At the same time drill hole locations were standardized on all sizes throughout the line so that lugs, holders, and other hardware would be drilled and attached exactly over the rivets for maximum concealment. The final stage of the rivet program, as it was called, provided for colored rivets to match the shell finish. It was all very artful and exciting and I thought gave us a leg up on the competition.

My emergency solution took off in the plant even though my staff embraced it with something less than enthusiasm.

The riveting was artfully concealed in new catalog illustrations and unfortunately the public, our drum public, accepted it with little to no enthusiasm. Apparently there were other suppliers of pyralin we didn't know about because our competitors, especially the overseas ones, did not seem to experience as much pearl shrinkage as we did. One part of my vaunted defense triad was crumbling! This gave me many sleepless nights.

My Son Reports For Work

My son, William F. Ludwig III, completed his education and reported for work about this time. I placed him under marketing director Frank Baxpehler as advertising manager. Here, under Frank's masterful tutelage, he learned more than in the previous years of formal schooling. In addition, Frank took him on many world tours, introducing him to the trade on their own turf. And Bill was a delight to all of the world of percussion and proved to be a mighty Ludwig ambassador of good will and confidence building.

On the other hand, since Bill was automatically a member of all company committeees and attended all meetings, I came under his increasingly questioning gaze and I began to feel exactly what my father must have

William F Ludwig III, William F. Ludwig II, 1984

felt. Bill was privy to my failings! I began to squirm and I felt more pressure to make profitable clever business decisions from the head of the conference table. Bill did not like the riveting program. I did. The trade ultimately did not like it either.

The Crucible Of Union Negotiations

Nowhere else but in employee relations is a chief executive officer judged by so many and so quickly. You are always under scrutiny– it never ends. And every CEO is under watch by the stockholders. In the case of Ludwig, the stockholders were family since it was a closely held corporation. It was a tremendous disappointment to my son when he attended his first union negotiations and felt the sting of open hostility and disagreement between our employees and management.

WFL Drum Company enjoyed over thirty years of amiable relations with labor. The contracts eventually covered not just one year, but three years before coming up for renewal, helping business continuity. In 1971, all of that changed when a radical chief steward was elected by the membership. He was a multi-lingual punch-press operator who had been thoroughly trained in the labor laws and labor organization.

We, on the other hand, were concentrating all of our efforts on building drums as opposed to the details of the labor laws. The result was that he tied us up in knots. He began publication of a monthly bulletin *Speak Out* in both Spanish and English. The introduction was "Dear Brothers and Sisters". That alone had tremendous appeal to our five hundred and fifty-five employees. The publication portrayed us as bumbling idiots who were grinding them down and taking advantage of them.

At my son's first negotiating meetings he was exposed to as much wrangling as he could stand. The situation put the lie to all the years I had told him I could handle union negotiations. All of a sudden Dad was outwitted at almost every turn and began to make very expensive settlements. Not just in actual productivity compensation, but in the matters of down time, or "pay without work" as it is often called. Time off with pay always costs the company extra and always adds to the costs of the products.

On the occasion of my Dad's 90th birthday four years earlier, I had put in place a profit-sharing plan in which a sizable slice of profits was credited to a separate fund for all employees. Apparently this did not buy labor peace with John Black, who was after more. Bear in mind that we were the only drum plant in the world with a labor union. That translated directly to the highest-priced drum company in the world! We were highly motivated to produce!

The situation seemed patently unfair to me. The union our workers belonged to, the AFL-CIO musical instrument workers, was too weak to organize any other drum companies because they had seen all the other plants they organized go out of business! I was distraught. My son was distraught. Sometimes I came home and felt like kicking the family dog! (Which happened to be a very large German Shepherd!) Every time a Union negotiation ended to narrowly avert a strike, we had to raise prices to cover our settlements. Our competitors watched us closely and, strangely enough, would raise their prices every time we did. Generally their increases were smaller, so I continued to hammer on quality.

Sabotage Rears Its Ugly Head

There are always some employees who want to vent their hatred by deliberately sabotaging the work. With our chrome-plated brass finishes as well as stainless steel, all it took was the scratch of a ring across the surface of one drum and an entire shipment would be stalled. This started to happen more and more frequently and we had no way to catch the perpetrators. We began to cover the more delicate finishes with heavy glue-backed paper which the dealer could peel off as part of the unpacking process. We were not alone. Sabotage was appearing in the automobile manufacturing business as well; random nuts and bolts were being dropped inside car bodies and hubcaps to produce rattles.

Our profit margins began to reflect this new revolting trend: 1974 sales were $19,528,000.00 with a 4.23% profit of $825,931.00. 1975 sales were $16,924,000.00 with a 2.7% profit of $466,635,000.00. The problem here is that as sales sink, profitability drops at an even more alarming rate because nearly all expenses remain the same. I could see that strong medicine would be required to reverse this trend and I turned to our controller for assistance. The controller, Mr. John Mahoney, had come aboard five years earlier and when I went to him for help, he immediately began to cut expenses. His cuts were everywhere; advertising, clinics, and all visible marketing expenses. The marketing and advertising people objected, of course, but this had to be done to bring percentages back into line. After all my years in business, I was still learning a basic (and bitter) lesson of economics: business is tough, and always ruled by profitability.

A Phone Call From Bill Crowden Changes My Life

Bill Crowden called one day to invite me to Berghoff's Restaurant in the loop to have lunch. The Berghoff is a venerable Chicago institution which celebrated its 100th year in business in 1998. For 100 years this elegant Bavarian-themed eatery has been very popular with downtown businessmen as a place to quietly conduct business over a first-class meal.

Dealers seldom call a major supplier without a good reason, so I assumed Bill had a serious concern. I immediately called meetings with the various departments Bill had contact with; sales, credit, returned goods, clinics, attempting to ascertain the reason for his invitation. I was sure that somewhere along the line someone had fouled up and I wanted to be prepared with an explanation and solution. Every department assured me that everything was fine with Crowden. I thought perhaps he just wanted to ask for a larger discount... or perhaps an exclusive selling territory?? I didn't sleep much that night and arrived at the office early the next morning filled with the greatest apprehension. What could he possibly want? With great dread, I plodded towards the Damen Avenue "L" (elevated train station) and arrived at the Berghoff early to secure a table for two in as quiet a location as I could. Bill arrived, and all through our German-style lunch he offered only light table conversation. I kept asking myself "when is he going to pop the question?" I sat on pins and needles as he made me wait until lunch was finished and the table cleared to pop the question. He asked for my daughter's hand in marriage!

First came relief that I did not have a serious business problem. *Then* came the thoughts that I couldn't think of a nicer man I would like my daughter to be married to. That is how deeply enmeshed in the drum business I was; it often took over my entire life, overshadowing even family relationships.

Bill Crowden and Brooke celebrate their engagement

I reached across the table with outstretched hand in full approval and literally skipped down the street on my way back to the office. To me this seemed like the makings of a perfect marriage; the drum maker's daughter betrothed to her father's largest local account. Bill was known all his life as a fine, honest, and, above all, hard-working man. I was in heaven and embraced my daughter as soon as I could. I passed the word through the plant that all was well with the Drums Unlimited account.

That union of Brooke and Bill produced two wonderful grandchildren, Marguerite and Will Crowden, who grew up to be outstanding citizens in the community. Today, thirty years later, the marriage continues rock-solid. I love them both and thank them for their wonderful children, our grandchildren.

The Great Decade Of Diversification

The urge to diversify was sweeping our nation. If you manufactured a specialty product, then you diversified into another (usually related) product to protect your base. Thousands of companies world-wide were suddenly busy getting into the other fellow's business. It became a mania. It touched me as well. One of the irritants we had to constantly put up with was fiber drum cases. Drums needed protection in transport and the fiber case was the answer; lightweight, strong, sized to fit each drum. From a distributing standpoint, there are problems, however. They are bulky and take up tremendous amounts of storage space. They literally surround air! The case companies manufactured cases in runs of each size, and often were not able to fill pending orders from the drum companies until they had enough orders to make it worth producing a batch of that size. When we were out of any given size, it meant we were unable to supply any complete set that included that size. It seemed I had lived a lifetime of frustration, never having the right size cases in stock to fill all the orders.

I decided to end that frustration by buying out my supplier, the Schuessler Case Company, and proceeded to do just that. Mr. Harold Schuessler was up in years and I used that as leverage to convince him to sell his company to me.

Wm. F. Ludwig Sr. and Mr. Schuessler signing the papers finalizing the Ludwig buyout of Schuessler Case Company

We agreed on a price. The deal was done, and in no time I received a call from Slingerland wanting to know their status with me as the new owner of their case supplier. I said the division would only be producing cases and timpani trunks for us, to which they replied s#@t and hung up.

The first thing I did was gather up all the dimensions of my competitor's cases and threw them all out. No longer would I be reliant on outside case suppliers! We kept the Schussler division in the same quarters it occupied at the time of the purchase until the lease ran out, then moved it to our new fourth floor at 2020 St. Paul Avenue; our newest and last plant addition.

With the Schuessler case acquisition we also acquired the timpani trunk manufacturing ability as well as the ability to make movie film transport cases and harp

trunks for harp maker Lyon & Healy. This provided us with a little diversification while solving our inventory problems. Mr. Schuessler stayed with me for a couple of years and then retired.

All through the late 1960s and early 1970s, Dick Schory had been busy with his own diversification plans. He brought in an electronics specialist, Bud Doty, and organized a new division, Ludwig Electronics. He developed an electric piano celeste in Building No. 4, utilizing bars from the Musser plant hung in a short-ranged upright piano cabinet made for us by a nearby piano manufacturer, the P.A. Starck Piano Company. We made a total of three hundred units, all under Bud Doty's supervision. Simultaneously, Dick contacted the Electro-Voice microphone people across the lake and made arrangements for us to distribute their microphones and electric hailers. We were given exclusive distribution of these products to the music store trade. Our sales force was delighted, since this represented new selling opportunities.

Then There Was Phase II

Dick made arrangements to present a Doty idea in electronics. The main marketing targets were guitar players, although it would enhance the sound of any instrument. The device was demonstrated to us in our board room by none other than the leading guitar player in town. The unit seemed quite attractive and we approved it for development as a form of diversification. The unit was dubbed the Phase II and was developed in building #4 on Willow Avenue. The concept expanded as the product developed, until it was a miniature synthesizer and was dubbed the Phase II Synthesizer. In its finished state it boasted of no less than a dozen buttons and lights and was about the size of a briefcase. The cost had developed significantly, as well, forcing up the retail price. We introduced it to the trade at $400.00 retail, and sold a few. Once again, the returned goods department brought in first one returned Phase II, then others, with electrical problems we had to fix for free. I was reminded over and over again of the words Phil Grant jotted in the margin of one our first Phase II ads, "Beware of anything you plug into the wall!" What a wonderful prophesy from an old friend who was also one of my competitors, for Phil Grant was the sales manager of the Fred Gretsch Manufacturing Company, maker of drums!

Finally I had to step in. I just had to discontinue production and let Bud Doty go. This infuriated Dick Schory who responded that we as a company didn't give it a chance. I had the same feelings toward the Phase II as I did toward the ElectroVoice microphones; we just could not repair them. I learned the hard way that a drum com-

company in Southern California. This company imbedded small light bulbs into a plastic tubing suitable for installation on floor steps in dark passages as well as drapes and curtains in night clubs.

Could we mount these lights in the interior of our very successful Vistalite plexiglass line? And would they not burn out quickly? Could they withstand the rigors of pounding that is the essence of drumming? These were the unanswered questions that only trial and error could solve. We set to work.

Within a month engineers had found a way to imbed the Lexon plastic tube into the joints between panels of multi-color or solid-colored Vistalite. Then came the electrical connections and transformer installations. The effect was beautiful. And best of all, the Lexon Company promised that these miniature bulbs would remain lighted for 16,000 years! I took them at their word. They probably will, but our less than perfect connections did not sustain that boast for more than a year at best.

I christened the new development "Tivoli" after the beautiful Tivoli Gardens of Copenhagen, Denmark. The initial set was sent down to the Holiday Inn club where Barrett Deems was appearing with Joe Venutti and his electric violin. On opening night I had the whole staff down and the drums looked gorgeous. Barrett Deems was so proud and I was busting my buttons. It was a very exciting time, and that evening made for a highly successful introduction of Tivoli lights.

The next morning at the office I received a very angry call from the manager of that club, ordering me to get the set out right away. The explanation he gave was that the lights overpowered the leader Joe Venutti and Joe had given the orders. He said, "They are the Joe Venutti quartet– not the Barrett Deems quartet!" This was a totally unforseen reaction and really torpedoed me right in the heart. It had never occurred to me that a *leader* would complain. That night I went down with my chief engineer and attached a dimmer to the system. I explained to Barrett that the lights would be dim until he soloed, then he was to reach down and flip a switch which would turn up the lights to full strength. The result of this quick fix was utter disaster as one can imagine. The last thing a drummer has to think about when embarking on a solo is flipping switches. The next day

pany cannot be an electronic company as well.

Dick Schory also steered me into buying out our advertising company which added to our overhead and did nothing to close the widening gap in our profit margin. Finally, I parted ways with Dick Schory and he continued his life in careers more suited to his flair for recording and electronics. Dick had been good to us and, as I related earlier, really organized and grew the concept of Total Percussion.

The Charms of Vistalite

One Christmas in the mid 1970s, Dick Gerlach, our wonderful sales manager, invited me out to a club he was playing during the holidays. Dick had draped strands of Italian lights around every tension handle on his bass drum and tom toms. His set was really lit up for the holidays! I was transfixed. The idea of lighted drum sets began to germinate in my mind, so I set the engineering department to work sourcing a company to supply us with miniature lights that we could lay inside the shells of an outfit. The result brought us to the Lexan

I went down and picked up that set. The Tivoli Vistalite was launched on an ill wind after a year of hard development work and thousands of dollars spent.

Still, that was only one upset. We continued on with the Tivoli Vistalite sales campaign and made up really beautiful brochures and catalog pages. One drummer even took the program a step further and installed triggers which lit up the set only on rim shots!

We introduced Tivoli sets at foreign trade shows across both oceans where the reception was better. Still we were plagued with electrical complaints and after a year we threw in the towel and called it quits for Tivoli Vistalite drum sets. There are still a few sets around, mostly for decoration. I know of one dealer of ours, Gary Asher at Nuncie's Music Company in Birmingham, Alabama, who has a Tivoli outfit in his office and it is a really fetching sight!

The 1973 Oil Embargo Strikes Us A Mighty Blow

Events half way around the world have a way of impacting us unexpectedly. The oil-producing countries of the near East halted oil shipments, raising the price of all oil globally. I didn't even realize that the plexiglass we used for Vistalite was an oil-based product, but I became acutely aware of that fact in very short order. Prices of the plexiglass sheets doubled, then doubled again. Literally overnight we started to lose money on all Vistalite drums even though we attempted to to raise

our prices to keep pace. Within six months we were forced to discontinue Vistalite drums completely and I lost one leg of my triad defense. To offset this disaster, we improved the equipment in our wood working section to improve the high gloss finishes on our main line of wood shell drums. We also switched over (at great expense) to heat-formed six-ply panels, electrically glued and flush butted using the very latest machinery. All of this took time and money– lots of it.

Russia Comes To Our Door

In the spring of 1977 a very excited Frank Baxpehler, my vice-president in charge of all exports, strode into my office waving some papers. As he tried to catch his breath, he informed me that the Russian government was buying a complete percussion line of instruments for the Moscow Philharmonic. Everything from triangles to Musser mallet instruments. Frank totaled the order at about $35,000 and it was to be a direct deal. The Russian government would be sending a delagation of first-chair musicians from the Philharmonic to visit us in addition to some other factories to inspect brass instruments such as trombones, trumpets, and french horns. I was aghast! What a compliment. They would consider no one but Ludwig and Musser for the percussion instruments including our finest hand-hammered balanced-action Symphonic model timpani. Frank explained that the paperwork was all in order, including a letter of credit

The new flat presses used to lay up plywood for the shells.

Circular molds for laying up shells.

91

for the $35,000. We were elated. With the rest of the paperwork was a request that we reserve two double rooms and a single at one of Chicago's medium-priced hotels on the near north side of Chicago's loop. The delegation was to include four musicians and a Commissar, Ganadney Sokoloff. One of the four was the principal timpanist of the orchestra. The rest were brass players, specializing in trombone, french horn, and trumpet.

They planned to visit Selmer for the trumpets and Holton for french horns. We entered the order and began to produce the instruments in anticipation of their visit in a months time.

In the middle of manufacturing this prestigious order, I received a request from our shop steward, John Black, to meet with the union committee regarding this order. I met with them, and by the time I had heard them out, I felt like exploding. The committee said they would call a work stoppage before they would allow anything more to be built for Russia. I was speechless. I first pointed out that a refusal to work would be a violation of our work contract with the union. Next, I reminded them of the fact that the Soviet system was entirely based on precepts that were pro-worker and anti-capitalism. They were looking at the situation backwards, I explained, and the way to forge peaceful relations with the Soviets was to supply them exactly the kind of products we had contracted to provide– musical instruments. "They are not going to strap these things around their waists and march against us to do battle," I preached. I spent two hours convincing them that the right thing to do was to fill the order using our usual high-quality workmanship and care, so they would admire rather than hate us. Finally one of the union men agreed, then another, but not John Black. I had to threaten him with a Federal Labor Board grievance filing. Under this threat and the cold eyes of his committee, he finally agreed to stop obstructing this transaction.

The big day arrived and I had the thrill of meeting my first Russians. The whole entourage came to the Ludwig factory. I later learned this was because they went everywhere as a group (under the supervision of the Commissar) to prevent any defections.

I had three sets of four timpani for the timpanist to play. I really enjoyed listening to him play through the percussion parts of the Russian literature, including a great deal of Tschaikowsky, my old favorite.

One night I entertained the group of Russians at my home, which has an adequate wet bar set up in my drum room. I hugely enjoyed socializing with them. After the fourth Vodka toast in fifteen minutes, we were fast friends! It was inconceivable that these guests could be considered the enemy.

Since it was springtime, I had them dump their overcoats in my bedroom when they arrived. At the same time I introduced them to our German Shepherd, Rex, and warned them that he was friendly but they should not touch him. After about two hours we decided to go out to eat. When we went to get their coats, the burly trombonist could not resist the temptation to hug Rex, who had made himself at home on their coats on my bed. In an instant, Rex raised up and bit him on the cheek. I was horrified and rushed to get my first aid kit. When I returned with it, Commissar Ganadney was already pouring straight vodka on the wound!

We had a wonderful evening of good will and friendship. The rest of the group teased the trombonist about his cheek wound, telling him that when he filled his mouth to play, the air would come out the hole in his cheek instead of the horn. (All conversation was in Russian, with Commissar Ganadney translating.)

After a most exciting week, the order was approved and shipped in heavy custom-built wooden crates for the long voyage to Russian and the Moscow Philharmonic.

The Triad Crumbles
Then stainless steel prices increased rapidly. This, together with the general marketplace rejection of this line, spelled disaster for the triad defense and in the mid 1970s, we were thrown back on our faithful wood line. With the new epoxy-sprayed finishes the wood line was well received by the trade.

My son William F. Ludwig III was now with me full time and we shared our triumphs and tragedies together, which was a great comfort.

The Name Drummer Scene Shifts
At about this time (the mid 1970s), drumming trends were changing. Public taste continued to dictate a need for "cool" music and the Big Band Era seemed to be history. Combos were in. There was one notable exception; Ed Shaughnessy who backed the Tonight Show with Doc Severinson's band. Tonight Show host Johnny Carson was the king of the nighttime TV shows, so the band's exposure was tremendous. I caught one of Ed's marvelous clinics and was at once captivated by his straightforward scholarly presentation complete with show cards and full explanations of his every move. He was born to teach and I thought, "We have to have him!" I negotiated a clinic tour arrangement with Ed and got him on the Ludwig bandwagon. That was the start of a nearly 30-year run until Carson retired and Jay Leno put together his own orchestra. Shaughnessy remains a Ludwig clinician and endorser!

Ed Shaughnessy

In the meantime, my son had found his calling in the rock field and all of the biggest shows that came to town would find him backstage hanging out with the great drummers of that era. He was following in my footsteps! Almost before I knew it, he had most of the biggest names signed up– about ninety drummers! It was truly amazing and wonderful to watch Bill work. Hours meant nothing to him. He was really inspired and everybody liked him– dealers, entrepreneurs, drummers, leaders. When anything went wrong with their gear, they knew all they needed was a phone call to Bill and the problem was resolved. Sometimes I saw his desk so piled up with telephone messages you could not even see the phone!

Thoughts Of The Company's Future

I have tried my best to explain how the Ludwig Drum Company was built. The title should have been the first indication to the reader that the story of the Ludwig Drum Company is my life story. There was no separating one from the other. The Ludwig Drum Company was more than a job, more than a career. I'm sure anyone who has read this far now understands that 1728 N. Damen Avenue was not an office I went to from 8 to 5 to collect a fat paycheck from a business my father handed me.

No business can afford to "coast" on past successes. I have often heard the maxim that every business is always in a state of change; it is either growing or shrinking. I felt that to be truer for our business than for most because of the many constantly changing factors.

First and foremost, there were the cultural factors.

The products in our catalog always had to reflect current "fads" in popular music. It was not enough to design and engineer a product, then balance manufacturing and marketing costs against dealer costs and retail prices. The process never ceased; our products had to be up to date!

How the products were distributed had to also be kept up to date. That meant constantly scrutinizing the effectiveness of distributors, sales organizations, and dealer networks.

Then there was the general economic landscape. An extreme example is what happened during the World Wars. A business owner must always be aware of the general economic climate; interest rates, inflation, discretionary income....

The savvy business owner must be able to quickly interpret how subtle changes in the general economic climate will translate into changes in the actual costs of operating his business; taxes, utilities, repairs, marketing, and the most significant expense of all, labor.

And let's not forget competition! (I wish I could!!) Competition is another area that is constantly changing and often limits a business owner's options!

I celebrated my 60th birthday in 1976. It was an exciting time to be in the drum business, and for all the challenges and stresses, I think it helped keep me young. Still, I could see that in 1981 I would be 65– the age of retirement for many. I had to ask myself how long I would be willing and able to keep this up. As the waters became more turbulent and challenging, my introspection became deeper.

As I said, my son had found his niche. He was spectacularly successful at a career that he found enjoyable and rewarding. I could not for a moment entertain the notion of asking him to assume responsibility for all of the decisions I had made over the last few decades. My father had built a drum company. I was named after him and I (with his help) built a drum company. My son carried the same name into a third generation and there are perhaps those who feel he should therefore have carried on and built or maintained a drum company. I am proud to say the family did not pressure him into such a decision.

CBS Comes Calling

This was, as I mentioned, the era of diversification. I started to get calls from outside the drum business asking if I might be interested in selling out. The first of these had been from Joe Grolimund, President of the Selmer Company in 1966. Joe had always loved drums and in an earlier portion of this story, I mentioned his start with us as advertising manager in the 1920s. Our discussions didn't really lead anywhere, since I was very preoccupied with building the business. Just a couple of years later his successor at Selmer, Jack Federson, made me an offer. I had to again refuse to consider it.

Joe Grolimund was President of the Selmer Co. in the 1960s when he suggested a merger with us. Little did I know then that this would happen twenty years later!

Every few years an offer would pop up, so I was not surprised when one day in 1976 I was approached by Robert Campbell with a buyout proposal. Campbell was President of CBS Musical Instruments, a division of the Columbia Broadcasting Company. It seemed odd to me that they were approaching me, since they already owned the Rogers Drum Company, which had given us a good run for our money! "Bob," I asked him, "You already have a drum company– why are you asking to buy me out?" "Well," he replied, "It isn't all that much of a company." I turned him down as politely as I could, but I often wonder what the outcome would have been if I had agreed.

Then came Charley Kaman of the Kaman Aircraft Company, manufacturers of helicopters for the Navy and a pioneer in wind generating machines for electrical energy production. They had diversified already and formed a musical instrument division. Charley flew in on his own corporate jet. Heady stuff for this drummer boy! We toured the plants and he made me very happy when I apologized for some of the older buildings, saying, "I like old buildings! They have character!" A few months later I flew to visit him at his corporate headquarters in Bloomfield, Connecticut. I learned that he would have to put the acquisition proposal through his board of directors since his was a publicly traded company. That would mean floating a stock issue, so nothing really developed out of his pursuit of me.

The stage was set for a telephone call from the Selmer Company in the spring of 1980. Selmer had been importing the Premier line from Britain. Rumor had it that they had a minority ownership interest in Premier. Mr. William Petersen, the President of Selmer, suggested that we stop being competitors. I was taken aback and curious as well, and invited him up for a visit. After an all-day visit of the facilities he said he would get back to me.

Selmer was the one company in the industry that I had an affinity for after all the years of contacts we had had, extending back to the 1920s. I conferred with my son, who agreed that we should listen up to see what

Paying out $2,800,000 from the profit fund to 555 employees on the occasion of the sale of the company.

Selmer had in mind. We were at the time heavily involved in Union negotiations and were experiencing strong competition from all sides. It was in this environment that we finally reached an agreement to sell out a year and a half later, on November 4, 1981. Selmer then sold off their 48% interest in Premier and assumed control.

The Selmer Years

Those first few days when I was no longer the boss were strange indeed. The new owner was very kind to me and my son, allowing us to stay on. I immediately gave up all control and responsibilities, and my hours became more relaxed. They did all the negotiating with customers, endorsers, and, of course, the Union, which I found to my liking. I promptly took my wife, daughter, and her husband Bill Crowden on an extended tour of Europe. We traveled from London across Europe to Venice on the famed Orient Express.

When after several weeks I returned, I found that a number of changes had been made, especially in the personnel area. Some of my best people had been discharged (with handsome severance packages) and many duties from various departments had been transferred to Indiana.

The Selmer Executive Vice President was put in charge of Ludwig and Musser and all divisions and he asked that I visit the universities from coast to coast to keep in touch with academia. This, of course, I was happy to do. I organized a drum lecture presentation titled *A History Of Percussion* which utilized color slides and antique drums, plus sound effects from my inherited collection. This lecture/demonstration took me to all corners of our nation and some foreign countries as well. The Selmer salesmen were very active in "booking" me and I enjoyed meeting hundreds of percussion people courtesy of the Selmer Company.

Catalano Arrives On The Scene

After several years of personnel changes during which I worked under no less than three marketing men, the company hired a first class drum man, James A. Catalano. A better choice could not have been made. I have hugely enjoyed working for Jim for almost twenty years now at numerous conventions and shows and stand in awe of his knowledge of percussion performance and the entire music industry from top to bottom. He is a highly motivated percussionist/businessman who has stepped up to assume responsibility as if he were the owner. At this time I can honestly say that I don't think there is anyone in the world who knows more about drums and the people in the industry than Jim. He has burnished the names of Ludwig and Musser. The Selmer executives made a wonderful choice when they made him their percussion marketing director and I look forward to many more years working with him.

My son did not care to stay with the company after it was restructured, as to do so would have involved moving to Elkhart. He now holds an important position with a huge accounting firm (the third largest in the world, with clients such as the State of Florida, U.S. Steel, and major automakers). He arranges all meeting facilities at the company headquarters in downtown Chicago, facilitating hundreds of meetings each week. He maintains an interest in drumming and visits his many professional drummer friends as they pass through Chicago. He is married to Lisa Ludwig and they are the proud parents of a daughter, Maggie Mae. Maggie Mae appears to have inherited the drumming gene; at the age of two she was picking up the sticks on her own and actually keeping time!

For twelve years I played in a local (Wheaton) municipal band and I still travel to conventions and lectures as of this writing in 2001.

It has been a long and interesting journey and I am blessed with continued good health and still on the road with my drum act. Maybe I'll run into you one day!

Wm. F. Ludwig II
July 12, 2001

My new boss, Jim A. Catalano, and I work a Drum Corps competition

Lisa and Bill Ludwig with Maggie Mae, in 2000

96

In 1987 Capital University of Columbus, Ohio, conferred an honorary Doctorate of Humantities Degree on Wm. F. Ludwig II.

Editor's note: It has been 20 years now since Mr. Ludwig sold his company to Selmer, and I find his relationship with the current Ludwig company quite remarkable. Think of it– two decades later and he is still attending drum shows, band director conventions, musical instrument expos... Drums, drum education, and the drum business are his lifeblood, not just interests he can walk away from after selling his company. His dedication and contributions have not gone unnoticed; his peers have bestowed numerous honors and awards in efforts to recognize this great man. The Percussive Arts Society inducted William F. Ludwig II into its hall of fame in 1993. His father was already a member, having been inducted in 1972. They are the only father-son members of this elite group with the exception of the world famous Zildjian cymbal making family. (Patriarch Avedis Zildjian was inducted in 1979, sons Armand and Robert were inducted in 1994 and 2000 respectively.)

Often in conversation you'll hear him refer to someone who "plays our drums" as if he is still personally responsible for the product. While he does not always agree with product or marketing decisions, his personal opinions (if they differ from the corporate line) remain confidential– always the gentleman.

Also in 1987, Selmer President H.W. Petersen presented Mr. Ludwig with a 50-year service pin. Petersen commented at the time of the presentation, "I've never had the privilege of awarding a 50-year pin before, and I'm sure that few others have, or, for that matter, ever will. Long before we acquired Ludwig Industries I admired you from afar– your energy, knowledge, and dedication. All of us have enjoyed working with you since joining forces in 1981."

A History Of Percussion

Pete Ryan, Executive Vice President of Selmer at the time that I sold the company, said to me, "And you, Ludwig, you go out to the Universities and maintain the Ludwig contact." I spent a great deal of time considering that directive. I thought to myself, "I just can't go out on campus and talk with these hot shot matched-grippers. I'm dated, and they're too busy. Furthermore, if they ask me to speak to their students, I'm surely going to come off as a pitiful old geezer."

Those thoughts led to the concept of a historical lecture. They cannot disagree with history!

Over the last twenty years, I have had the pleasure of delivering my presentation nearly two hundred times in thirty-eight states and ten foreign countries.

This performance took place in April 1987 in Holland. Dutch distributor Edwin Klaus is reading the script.

The reader will get an idea of what my presentation includes by reading the article originally printed in *The Instrumentalist*, which follows these notes. The presentation is livened up with actual playing demonstrations. I demonstrate historical military command signals on my rope drum, and sometimes enlist the aid of competent attendees for multi-drum signals such as *Three Camps*.

The drummers' "traps" are always a crowd favorite. The presentation concludes with the actual performance of a script from the early days of radio. Audience members are enlisted to read the script and help operate contraptions such as the steam locomotive imitation, horses hooves, the sure-fire blank shot holder, the cricket and cuckoo imitators, etc.

The trap assortment, laid out for a lecture presentation.

A History Of Percussion

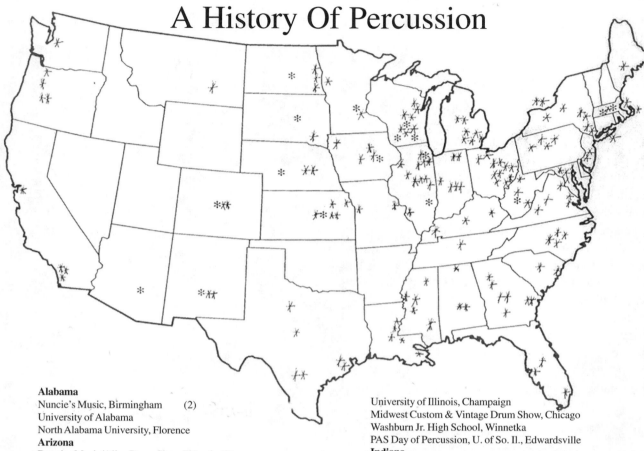

Alabama
Nuncie's Music, Birmingham   (2)
University of Alabama
North Alabama University, Florence
Arizona
Boggies Music/Alley Drum Shop, Phoenix (3)
Arkansas
Wallick Music Company, Pine Bluff
Arkansas State University, Jonesboro
California
National Association of Music Merchants, Anaheim
Nat'l Assoc.of School Music Dealers, San Diego (3)
Nat'l Assoc. Band Instrument Repair Technicians
Drum World, San Francisco
Canada
Vintage Drum Association Show, Toronto (2)
Colorado
Rupp's Drum Shop, Denver
Rocky Mtn.Music Dealers, Colorado Springs (2)
Florida
Florida State University, Gainesville
University of South Florida, Tampa
University of Miama, Coral Gables
Georgia
All State Band Festival, Savannah
Galaxy Music Company, Stone Mountain
Coastal Heritage Society, Savannah (2)
Georgia State University, Atlanta
Great Southern Music Co. Day of Percussion, Rydal
Kennesaw College Day of Percussion, Marietta
University of Georgia, Athens
Illinois
Bands of America World Percussion Symposium
Bradley University, Peoria
Chicago Federation of Musicians, Chicago
Eastern Illinois University, Charleston
Midwest Band Clinic, Chicago
Moline High School, Moline
PAS Day of Percussion, Elmhurst College
Pro-Am Music Company, Darien
Skins & Tins Drum Shop, Champaign

University of Illinois, Champaign
Midwest Custom & Vintage Drum Show, Chicago
Washburn Jr. High School, Winnetka
PAS Day of Percussion, U. of So. Il., Edwardsville
Indiana
American Musical Instrument Society, Elkhart
Drum Center of Indianapolis (2)
Central High School, Elkhart
State University, Terre Haute
Paul-Mueller Percussion Studio, Indianapolis
Iowa
Coe College, Cedar Rapids
Iowa Bandmasters Assoc. Convention, Des Moines
Northern Iowa University, Cedar Falls
Spencer High School, Spencer
PAS Day of Percussion, Grinnell College
Kansas
Kansas Bandmasters Association, Wichita
University of Kansas, Lawrence
Wichita State University, Wichita
Kentucky
Morehead State University, Morehead
University of Kentucky, Lexington
Louisiana
Fransen's Drum Shop, New Orleans
Louisiana State University, Baton Rouge
Prof. Erny's Music Company, Lafayette
Northeastern Louisiana University, Monroe
Southeastern Louisiana University, Hammond
Maryland
The Drum Cellar, Bethesda
Bill's Music House, Glen Bernie Park
MD. Day of Percussion, Towson State University
University of Maryland, Baltimore
Maine
Portland Music Center
Massachusetts
Cape Cod Music Festival, Hyannis Port
Interntl. Assoc. of Rudimental Percussionists, Boston
Center Street Drums, Boston

Danvers High School, Danvers
Joe's Drum Shop, Beverly
Michigan
Carty's Music Inc., Ypsilanti
Christian Music, Grand Rapids
Central Michigan University, Mt. Pleasant (2)
Interntl. Assoc. of Jazz Record Collectors, Detroit
Stearns Collection, U. of Michigan, Ann Arbor
Michigan Day of Percussion, U. of M. at Midland
University of Michigan
Minnesota
Luthern Summer Music Camp, Moorhead
Nels Vogel Music Co., Fargo
Winona State College Day of Percussion, Rochester
Red Wing College
Mississippi
Jackson State University, Jackson
Tupelo High School, Tupelo
University of Southern Mississippi, Hattiesburg
University of Mississippi, Oxford
Valley State University, Itta Bena
Missouri
Explorers Percussion Drum Shop, Kansas City
Missouri Day of Percussion, St. Louis
P.A.S. International Convention, St. Louis
University of Missouri, Kansas City
Montana
Montana Day of Percussion, Billings
Nebraska
Dietz Music Company, Lincoln
Luthern Summer Music Camp, Lincoln
New Jersey
P.A.S. Day of Percussion, Trenton College, Trenton
N.J. State Music Educators, Cherry Hill
New Mexico
Allegro Music Co., Santa Fe
Luchetti Drum & Guitar Shop, Albuqurque
The Music Box, Las Cruces
New York
Drome Sound, Schnectady
Eastman School of Music, Rochester
Long Island Day of Percussion, Plainview
Long Island Drum Center, Long Island
N.Y. Educators Assoc. Convention, Kiamesa Lake
Percussion Paradise, Staten Island
KOSA Percussion Camp, Potsdam
U.S. Military Academy, West Point
North Carolina
Kings Mountain High School, Kings Mountain
McFayden's Music Co., Greenville
North Charlotte High School, Charlotte
Reliable Music Co., Charlotte
North Dakota
Luthern Summer Music Camp, Moorhead
Marguerite's Music Store, Moorhead
North Dakota Music Educators Assoc., Gd. Forks
University of Mary, Bismark
Ohio
Bill's Music Center, Ashland (2)
Capital University, Columbus
Coyle Music Co., Columbus
Coffman Music Co., Marietta
Coffman Music Co., Lancaster
Columbus Pro Drum Shop, Columbus
Fostoria High School, Fostoria
Kent State University, Akron
Lentine Music Co., Akron
Marion Cadets Drum & Bugle Corps, Marion
Ohio Music Educators State Convention, Columbus
Ohio University, Athens
Sandusky High School, Sandusky

Warren Music Co., Warren
Zampino's Drum Shop, North Canton
Oregon
Rickett's Music Store, Roseburg
Western International Band Conference, Ashland (2)
Western Oregon State Conference, Portland
Pennsylvania
Duquesne University, Pittsburgh
Haines Music Co, Selingsgrove (2)
Northwest Pennsylvania Music Festival, Erie
P.A.S. Day of Percussion, Lock Haven
Puerto Rico
Inter-American University, Mayaguez
South Carolina
South Carolina Dand Director's Assoc., Charleston
South Carolina Day of Percussion, Sumter
South Dakota
Luthern Summer Music Camp, Sioux Falls
Shrine To Music, Vermillion
Tennessee
Austin Peay University, Clarksville
Memphis State University, Memphis
Stoltz Music Co., Memphis
Taiwan
Adolphus Music Co., Taipei
Laurel University
University of Taiwan, Taipei
Texas
Brook Mays Music Co., Dallas
H & H Music Co., Houston
North Texas State University, Denton
Texas Bandmasters Assoc. Convention, San Antonio
University of Houston, Houston
Virginia
Armed Forces School of Music, Norfolk
Fifes & Drums of Yorktown Association, Yorktown
James Madison University, Harrisonburg
Antique Drum Show, Roanoke
P.A.S. Virginia/DC State Meeting, Annandale
Washington
Corby's Music House, Charleston
Jefferson High School, Shenandoah Junction
Music Educators Association, Huntington
Southern West Virginia Day of Percussion, Concord
Wisconsin
Casio Music Company, New Berlin
Carroll College Day of Percussion, Waukesha
Heid Music Company, Green Bay
Lawrence University, Appleton
Monroe High School Fine Arts Festival, Monroe
University of Wisconsin, Green Bay
University of Wisconsin, Oshkosh
Ward Brodt Music Company, Madison
University of Wisconsin, Madison
P.A.S. State Meeting, Madison
Drum Guild, Wauwatosa
Denmark
Copenhagen Drummers Club
Holland
Encheness Conservatory of Music, Encheness
Conservatory of Music, The Hague
Utrecht Conservatory of Music, Utrecht
Sweden
Royal Conservatory of Music, Stockholm
Norway
Oslo Conservatory of Music
Belgium
Westerlo Drummer's Club, Westerlo
Japan
Nonaka Boito Company Executives, Tokyo
Nonaka Boito Company Headquarters, Yokohama

This article was excerpted from Wm. F. Ludwig II's slide lecture "A History of Percussion" and published in this form in the November, 1990, edition of "The Instrumentalist".

A History of American Drumming
by William F. Ludwig, II

On the morning of April 19, 1775 William Diamond strapped on his drum, stepped onto the village commons, and sounded the alarm of the American Revolution. Later that morning British troops fired on the 69 volunteers he summoned, but Diamond escaped, and his drum is now in a Boston Museum. Two and a half months later drummers on both sides beat cadences to steady the troops as they closed for battle on Bunker Hill.

The drums gave order to the chaos of the battlefield. In the din of musket and cannon fire the drummers sounded calls that could be heard by the troops. While the human voice penetrates only a few hundred yards, the sound of the drum carries for a quarter to half mile. George Washington insisted that at least one drummer be assigened to every

With a marching tempo of only 90 steps per minute, drummers fashioned intricate patterns called fillings between the beats. Today these fillings appear in many modern percussion books as paradiddles, flam accents, and double drags. These early cadences were the beginning of our present rudimental system and were written with left-hand strokes with stems pointing up while stems for right-hand strokes pointed down. Drummers played all hollow notes pianissimo, solid ones fortissimo, and solid notes with a slash mezzo fortissimo. Slowly American drummers perfected the new notation of the calls and cadences and passed them through the regiments of the growing Continental Army.

George Frederick von Steuben, an aristocratic Prussian whom Washington made Inspector General to the Conti-

marching unit to provide the cadence to move the men in an orderly fashion. He used the drum to set the time of camp activities throughout the day. The first of these distinctive calls was "Reveille", which drummers performed as soon as they could see a tree at 1,000 paces in the early morning light.

nental Army, ordered a drum factory set up in Philadelphia and three artisans produced 399 military rope drums for regimental drummers. By contrast, however, one ship sailing from England provided the British with 760 drums.

The Revolutionary War barrel drums were enormous by today's standards and had shells measuring 18 inches, by

The Drummer Of Valley Forge

the event of a surprise night attack. The three camps were a minimum of a half mile apart, and drummers soon developed a system of calling back and forth before 'Taps" with a series of continuous five- ten- and eleven-stroke rolls. A drummer in one camp would begin playing the first section of "Three Camps" followed by the second section played by the drummer in the next camp. Both drummers waited for the drummer in the third camp to check in. If a British drummer familiar with the piece broke in, the Americans would know it by the style of his drumming and sound the alarm. Still in use today, "Three Camps" is a marvelous solo that shows the solid nature of the rudimental system.

When leaving or entering camp, companies and regiments marched to drum cadences, but in open country drummers released the tension from their drum heads and carried their instruments by the ceremonial sash cords until marching into the next campsite when they resumed playing cadences.

Von Steuben's infantry manual of 1778 prescribed drum and fife practice from 10:00 a.m. until 1:00 p.m. each day in camp. Young drummers taught by older hands memorized dozens of calls and cadences until they could be played on demand of the commanding officer. At dawn's first light the duty drummer sounded "Drummer's Call," which was the signal for all company drummers to report to the regiment and sound enmasse "Reveille" at dawn. 'Cfficer's Call" and 'Breakfast Call" soon followed. For dinner call fifers and drummers sounded "Roast Beef", so named because the army issued each infantryman a slab of raw beef to cook on the end of a pointed stick. For today's drummer "Roast Beef", with its double drags, is an excellent exercise. The last call of the day was "Taps". Six evenly spaced slow taps, the first f, the second p, were repeated twice. Thus, from sun up to sun down the drum governed every moment of the field soldier's day.

Drums and fifes were an integral part of the surrender ceremony at Yorktown. "Yankee Doodle", originally in-

17 inches across, and an overall height of 22 inches to provide maximum volume. Constructed of solid beechwood or maple panels, drum shells were soaked in water and then steamed and bent into their circular shape. The two-inch-high hoops were of half-inch thick straight-grained maple to withstand the rigors of field use, and drum heads were tanned calfskin, while the snare or lower head was tanned from unborn calfskin. Lamb gut snares provided a crisp sound and action but were affected by weather and humidity changes unless heavily shellacked. Drum sticks of this period were thick. and heavy. When squeezed down by the drummer, leather tugs around the shell applied tension to both heads simultaneously. This method of tightening both drum heads at once persisted into the mid-19th century when J. Dermond developed independent tensioning. Spare sash cord was braided to hang below the drum for decoration, but drummers often used it to replace frayed and worn segments of the regular tensioning cord. Because taut skin heads often cracked with changes in temperature or humidity, drummers relaxed the rope tensioning whenever the drum was not in use.

In section 21 of his field manual, Von Steuben ordered all large bodies of troops to form three separate camps in

vented by the British fifers and drummers as a derisive song for the bumpkins of the American colonies, was tauntingly played by the Americans as the British troops threw their guns to the ground.

In the War of 1812 drummers controlled the loading and firing of artillery batteries. After each volley a cloud of smoke enveloped the cannoneers and they could not see the artillery's controlling officer. To avoid confusion drummers rolled loudly until ordered to stop by the artillery officer lowering his saber. Upon hearing the roll cease, the artilleryman fired a round. If drummers resumed rolling the men reloaded the cannon and waited for the roll to stop before firing again. If there were no drum roll after a round was fired, the troops moved the battery to another location.

In the first 90 days of the Civil War, drummers, fifers, and bands paraded to attract volunteers in a form of recruitment termed marching to the drum because enlistees often signed the Papers of Fidelity on a drum head. All Northern States sent musical units with their enlistees. Neither their uniforms nor musical instruments matched, but eventually the Department of War standardized both, settling on a rope-tensioned field snare 12 inches deep by 15 inches in diameter. The Revolutionary War's barrel drum was abandoned because the marching cadence increased to over 100 steps per minute in the 50 years separating the wars, and drummers wanted a more manageable field drum with a crisp, higher-pitched sound. Jos. Rogers & Son, the J.W. Pepper Co., and other Union drum nvanufacturers produced 64,000 eagle drums, each emblazoned with the Great Seat of the United States.

At the War's beginning drummers were adults, but as the conflict dragged on and casualties mounted, they were ordered from musical units to serve as combat troops. Young boys who had left their homes to follow the army and perform camp duties soon enlisted as drummers and received uniforms. These camp followers became skilled in rudimental proficiency because their light duties allowed for several hours of practice each day. Their newly achieved status, however, lost its glamour on the battlefield: many young drummers broke rank and ran in the heat of combat, leaving their units without a means of communication. To avoid this, officers sometimes tied young drummers to their braided sashes and dragged them into battle. By the end of the War both sides had used drummers younger than 10 years of age.

During the war over-the-shoulder slings gradually replaced neck slings, and drummers carried their instruments against their left leg; this allowed the right hand, which is usually stronger, to bring the bead of the stick flat against the head. If the stick came down at too much of an angle it would split the head with the tip of the bead.

Drummers always marched to the right in the front rank alongside the officer and the color bearer. All three were prime targets for enemy sharpshooters who could stop an infantry's advance by knocking out any one of them. Without the sight of the colors or the sound of the drum, an attack would falter. In an average advance across 500 yards,

6 or 7 color bearers would be shot, but another soldier would, immediately pick up the colors and restore the forward momentum.

This was the first war in which camp entertainment consisted of fifers and drummers performing popular tunes and playing the troops to sleep each night. Official reviews and parades were popular in-this era; there were long periods between campaigns in which drummers and fifers provided pageantry for the popular parades and when the War was finally over, 250,000 soldiers marched down Pennsylvania Avenue to the cadence of eagle drums.

With the demobilization of the Civil War armies, the U.S. Government formed large cavalry regiments to protect the westward-bound wagon trains. With the use of a bugle a cavalry soldier could sound signal calls while still controlling his mount. Thus, the drum, which was the instrument of choice within the ranks of armies for centuries, was displaced by the compact little horn. By 1868 the drum became the instrument of pure entertainment that it is today.

Because the government allowed returning Civil War veteran drummers to keep their instruments, thousands of small community bands and dance orchestras formed. A dance drummer of this time would set his snare drum on a chair in front of him (the snare drum stand was not invented yet) and place his bass drum at a right angle to it.

Replica of a Revolutionary War field drum, the
Liberty **model, made by the Cooperman Drum Co.**

The Battle of Bunker Hill

He'd tap the bass drum with his snare stick on the down beat and his snare on the after beats on polkas, waltzes, quadrilles, and standard 2/4 marches. This arrangement worked well as long as the dance music remained fairly straightforward.

On February 1, 1887 George R. Olney changed all this by patenting the first bass drum foot pedal. Drummers were now free to use both hands for snare performance. Following Olney's breakthrough came a number of devices that transformed the drum from a military instrument to one used for entertainment. Olney's bass drum pedal, E.E. Fry's throw-off snare drum strainer, wire brushes by L. Allis and A.R. Wines and the low-boy sock cymbal pedal invented by Dixieland drummer Vick Berton, show particular genius and have changed the way we use percussion instruments.

The development of the bass drum pedal enabled one man to perform the function of three players by combining bass, snare drum, and cymbals all under one command. Small groups of five players gathered around the new set up of drums and performed marches, polkas, and waltzes to the steady beat of one drummer instead of three. Bass drum stabilizers soon made an appearance and eventually took the form of small spurs attached to the drum's lower counterhoop. Until their development a bass drum would roll over on it's side if accidentally touched in the wrong place.

Another primary invention of the mid-19th century was the development of the first separate tention drum, which enabled drummers to control the tension on the heads independently of each other. The first patent for this instrument was issued on February 3, 1863 to J. Dermond. His invention consisted of nothing more dramatic than fastening two cut-down rope tension drums together allowing separate tension applications to the batter head as well as the tender snare head. These separate tensioned drums arrived too late for use in the Civil War, but afterwards the J.W. Pepper Drum Co., one of America's earliest full-production drum manufacturers, replaced the rope of the Dermond separate tension drum with metal rods and variations of this model are produced today.

A year after Berton's invention of the low-boy sock cymbal, Barney Walberg of Worcester, Massachusetts, added a 32-inch extension and brought the cymbals up to their present hi-hat position. At the time of the invention cymbals had a deep-cupped shape resembling the profile of a formal dress high hat. This last development gave us the drum set that we still use today.

Prior to 1927 all movies were without sound, and theater owners employed musicians to accompany the action o the flickering screen. Drummers brought their drums and contraptions, soon shortened to traps, to do this. A single movie of that era could call for as many as 120 different sound effects from the drummer, who carried the massive array in a steamer trunk. Often drummers would trade sound effects with one another to balance their inventory.

Most movie houses supplied the public with six shows each day, and because the projectionists had to rewind a reel of film by hand before they could start another one, live performing acts were featured between each movie. Percussionists' work never stopped; at the end of a week's run, they spent an all-night session lining up sound effects for the following week's bill, and learning every leg kick, rim shot, and sound effect for the live acts. Of course, with the introduction of talking movies in the late 1920s, live acts at movie houses came to an end.

America's history in the early years was guided by the development of drums. I doubt that armies could have marched and fought without the indispensable aid of the drum and those drummer boys of long ago. Then as now, we applaud the drum's importance on history's musical stage.

The oldest drum in the author's collection, a Porter Blanchard rope drum made in 1812, has been donated to the Chicago Historical Society.

A few of the other rope drums from the author's personal collection.

FAMILY PHOTOS

Johanette (Dietrich) Ludwig
1849–1932
Matriarch of the Ludwig family whose personal savings often saved the business in the teens and early 1920s.

Mother Elsa in her costume for the Chicago Grand Opera Company.

Elsa Maria (Gunkler) Ludwig
1893–1958
Mother Elsa owned the building at 1728 N Damen Ave. The rent was $750.00. We were often in arrears!

Wm. F. Ludwig II (age 10), Bettie Ludwig (age 6) with dog "Toy". The 1001 Maple St. home in Evanston, Illinois, had a big back yard in which we played. Years later I purchased my home in Oak Brook primarily for its back yard for my growing family.

Brooke Ludwig at Interlochen
age 13.

FAMILY PHOTOS

Maggie and Valentine– one of many pets in our lives
including other cats and two German Shepherds.

Rex

Wm II, Maggie, Brooke, Wm III
The whole family turned out full force to battle for drum
orders at the Frankfurt, Germany, spring trade fair– an
international event!

Maggie and Brooke

FAMILY PHOTOS

Bettie with Bing Crosby, 1944 USO Tour

Bettie was assigned to the midshipmen school at Notre Dame University where she met her future husband Lt. James R. Dodson. She was an experienced secretary to the Admiral.

Bettie with Dad and her daughter Pat, (left)

Sister Bettie Dodson, Bill and Brooke Crowden, Bill Ludwig III, Maggie at their shining best at one of many trade shows.

With granddaughter Marguerite
Crowden, Age 2

Brooke with her children Will Crowden and Marguerite.

Marguerite (25) and Will (21) Crowden in 2001,
on holiday trip to Salzburg, Austria.

Three generations in 1980. Maggie
Ludwig with daughter Brooke
Crowden on left and Marguerite
Crowden in garden at home.

The Crowden family in 1997. (L-R) Will,
Brooke, Marguerite, Bill

FAMILY PHOTOS

Brother and sister pound out their famous duet taught by Herman Wiegman.

The three generations of Ludwigs as featured soloists at a music convention.

111

WM. F. LUDWIG II, WORLD TRAVELER

On the road down Mexico way for a clinic in Mexico City

In Belize (formerly British Honduras), mixing some sport while searching for Rosewood logs (below) for marimba and xylophone bars.

When the Chicago Symphony toured Europe, I tagged along. Here I pose with CSO percussionists Al Payson on the left and Gordon Peters on the right in Vienna, Austria.

Wm II and Maggie attending the opera at the Festspiele house in Bayreuth, Germany.

WM. F. LUDWIG II, WORLD TRAVELER

The author and Bill Crowden crossing the English Channel on the way to the French version of the Orient Express.

Mr. and Mrs. William Crowden on the Orient Express en route to Italy

Maggie and the author boarding the Orient Express

Relaxing in Venice. No more Unions, phone calls, bills to pay!!

INDEX

A Message From Jim Catalano,
Ludwig Marketing Manager, 2001

Just like many of you reading this book, I grew up with the Ludwig Drum catalog at my side. I knew all the products, model numbers, specs, and dreamed of all the possibilities. I looked up to the Ludwig family with admiration for making such creative and high quality percussion products. That feeling never changed through my years of college and professional life as an active working percussionist.

The idea of one day working for the Ludwig Drum Company was only a dream, but that dream became reality for myself. After receiving my masters from The University of Notre Dame, I worked as a high school band director. Then, in 1978, an opportunity came along to work in the music industry when Selmer owned a percentage of The Premier Drum Company. This was an eye opening experience and I witnessed first hand the dynamics of Ludwig as one of their competitors.

The world is in constant change, and Selmer eventually purchased Ludwig in late 1981. By early 1983, I was offered the marketing position with the Ludwig Drum Company, and it changed my life. I'll always remember that first day on the job when I met the man whose pic-

ture I had always seen on the inside front cover of the Ludwig catalogs. Bill Ludwig II was very impressive. Although technically retired by this time, he was still very active with the company. I vowed right then and there to keep it that way, as long as he was willing and able. So now, twenty plus years later and counting, Bill Ludwig continues as an active lecturer and personality with the Ludwig Drum Company and in the percussion industry.

Bill became a personal friend, and my respect for him grew. I coined a new nickname for him: "The Chief". After all, he is the patriarch of our company. His leadership through the forties, fifties, sixties, and seventies established Ludwig has one of the most dynamic companies in the entire music industry. They branded the Ludwig name so well that even people who were not drummers knew about Ludwig. Now, many of his friends call him "The Chief".

Taking on the responsibility to lead Ludwig through the eighties, nineties, and into the new century has been a challenging task. But I always knew I had the confidence and support of "The Chief" behind me. In the business world, there are few instances where the former owner stays active with the company he sold and plays a vital role. Well, Bill Ludwig II has done just that. He continues to attend shows, give lectures on the history of percussion, and now he has put the wonderful story down for all to read from his perspective.

Today Ludwig is a major player in the percussion industry. Ludwig Educational Percussion Kits are usually the first impressions young students have of our products and company. From there, we supply the combo market with drum outfits and related drums and percussion accessories with a full range of quality and price ranges to meet the market's needs.

Our factory in Monroe, North Carolina, is well managed and continues to manufacture professional quality drums with maple and birch shells and snare drums in both wood and metal shells. We also manufacture marching and concert drums as well as our own Weather Master Drumheads, mallets, and many percussion accessories.

Bill passed the symbolic keys to his company on to my colleagues and myself many years ago, and we vowed to keep the drums, legend, and tradition alive and growing for future generations. We are so grateful to Bill Ludwig II for his vision, dedication and passion for this business. Ludwig, *The Making of a Drum Company,* is an American success story. We move forward with the same dedication and passion instilled into us by our leader, "The Chief". I invite you to check us out at your favorite drum shop or music store, at one of the many shows we exhibit at annually, or on the worldwide web at www.ludwig-drums.com.

  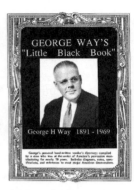

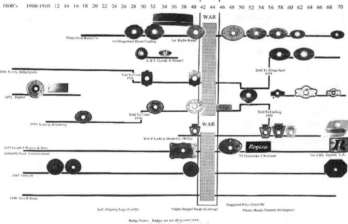